20 Double-Sided, Color-Coordinated, Designer Papers in 8x10 Inch, Non-Perforated, Book Style

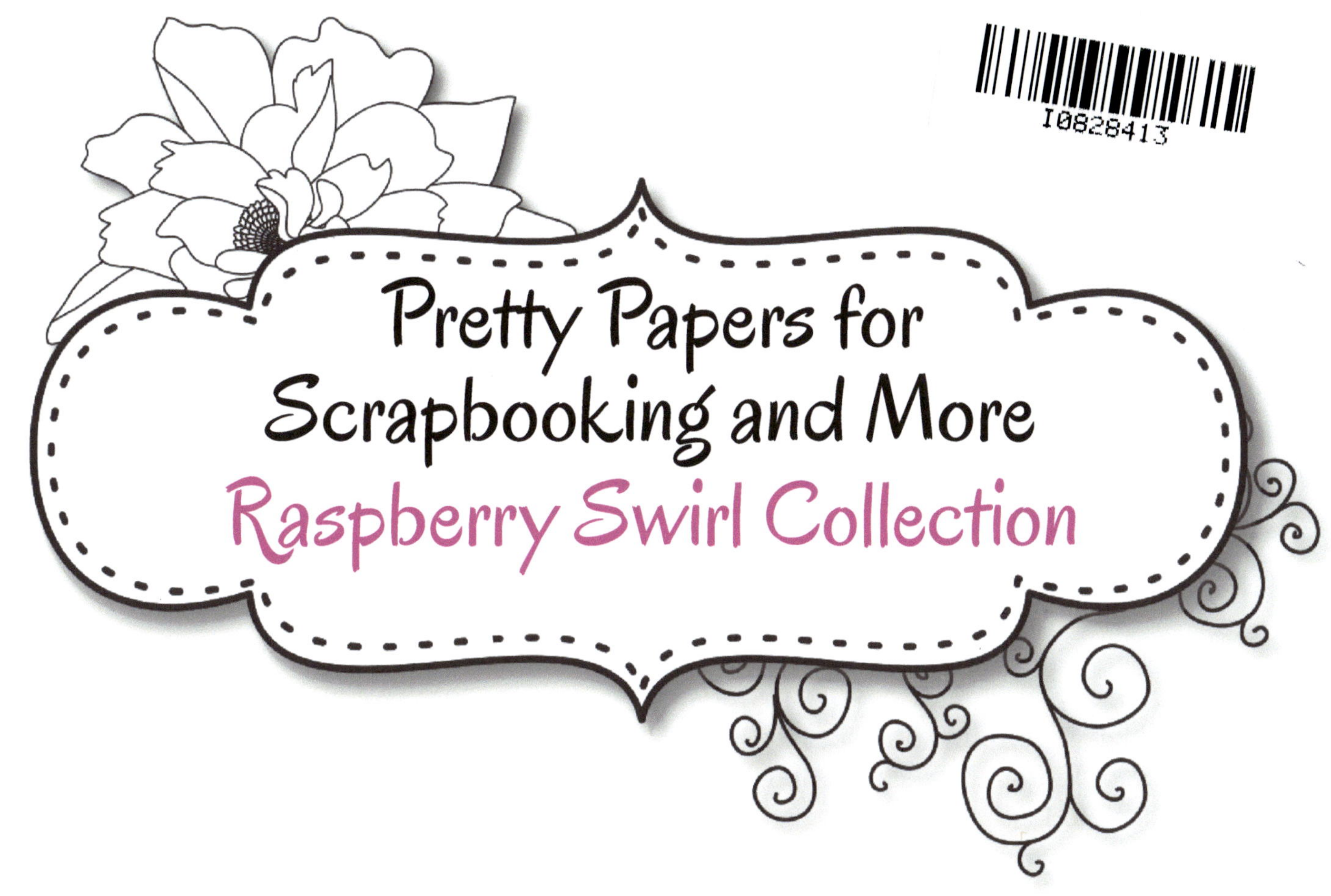

Share Your Brilliance Publications
Hartford, CT

Published by Share Your Brilliance Publications
A Division of Vibrant Marketing Publications.

ShareYourBrilliancePublications.com

Printable paper packs and more available at:
ShareYourBrilliance.com
ShareYourBrilliance.etsy.com

ISBN 978-1-947158-20-7

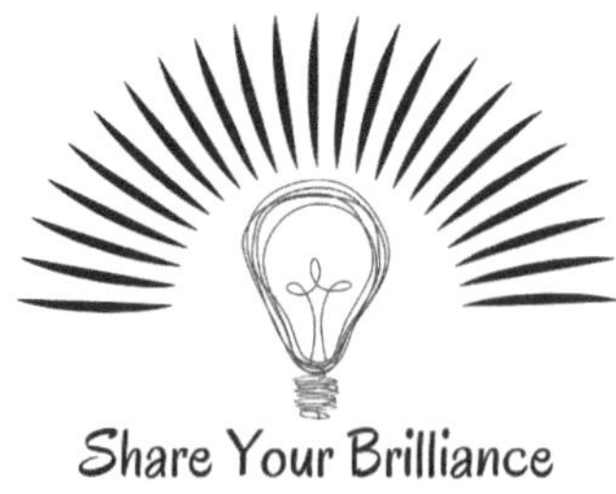

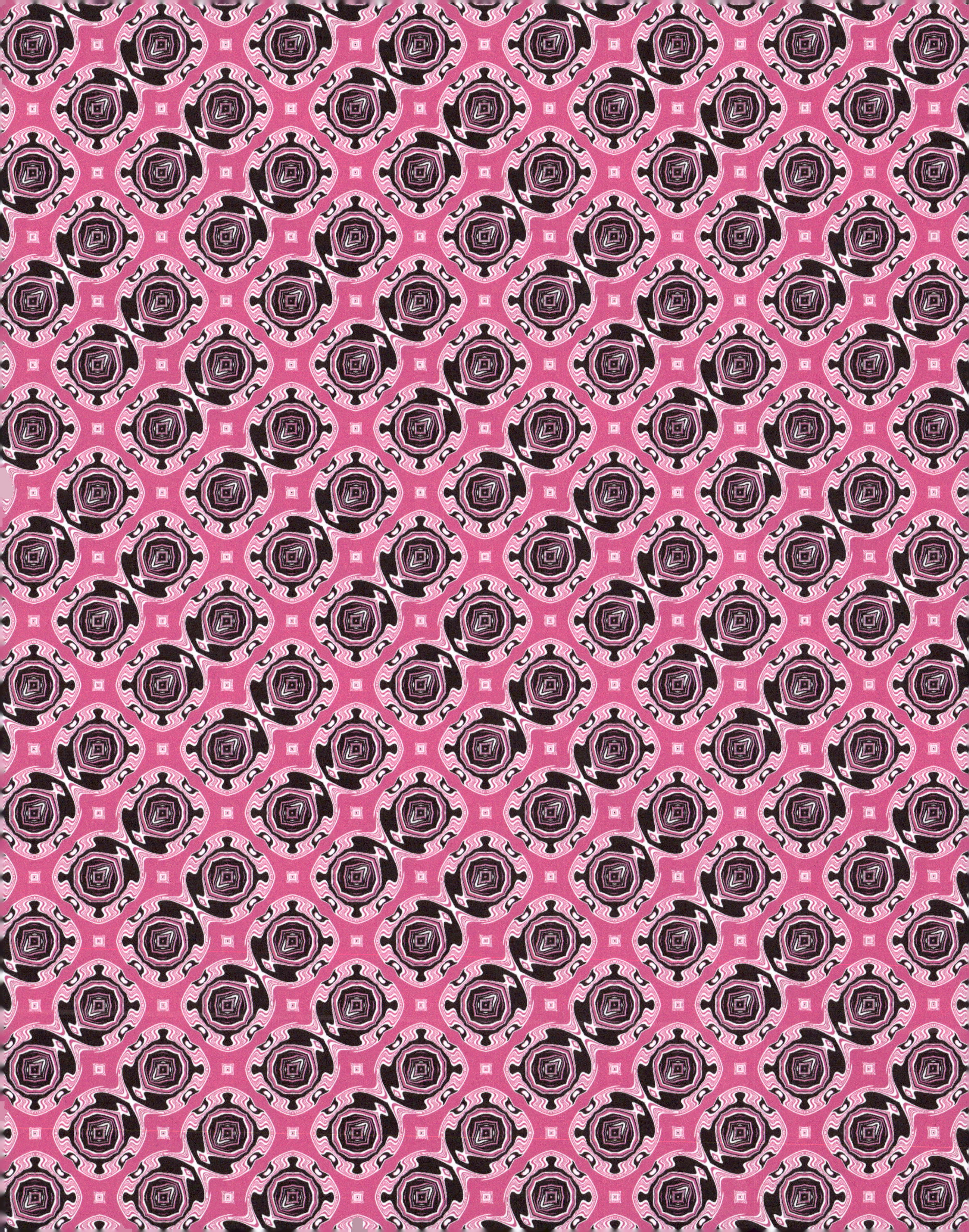

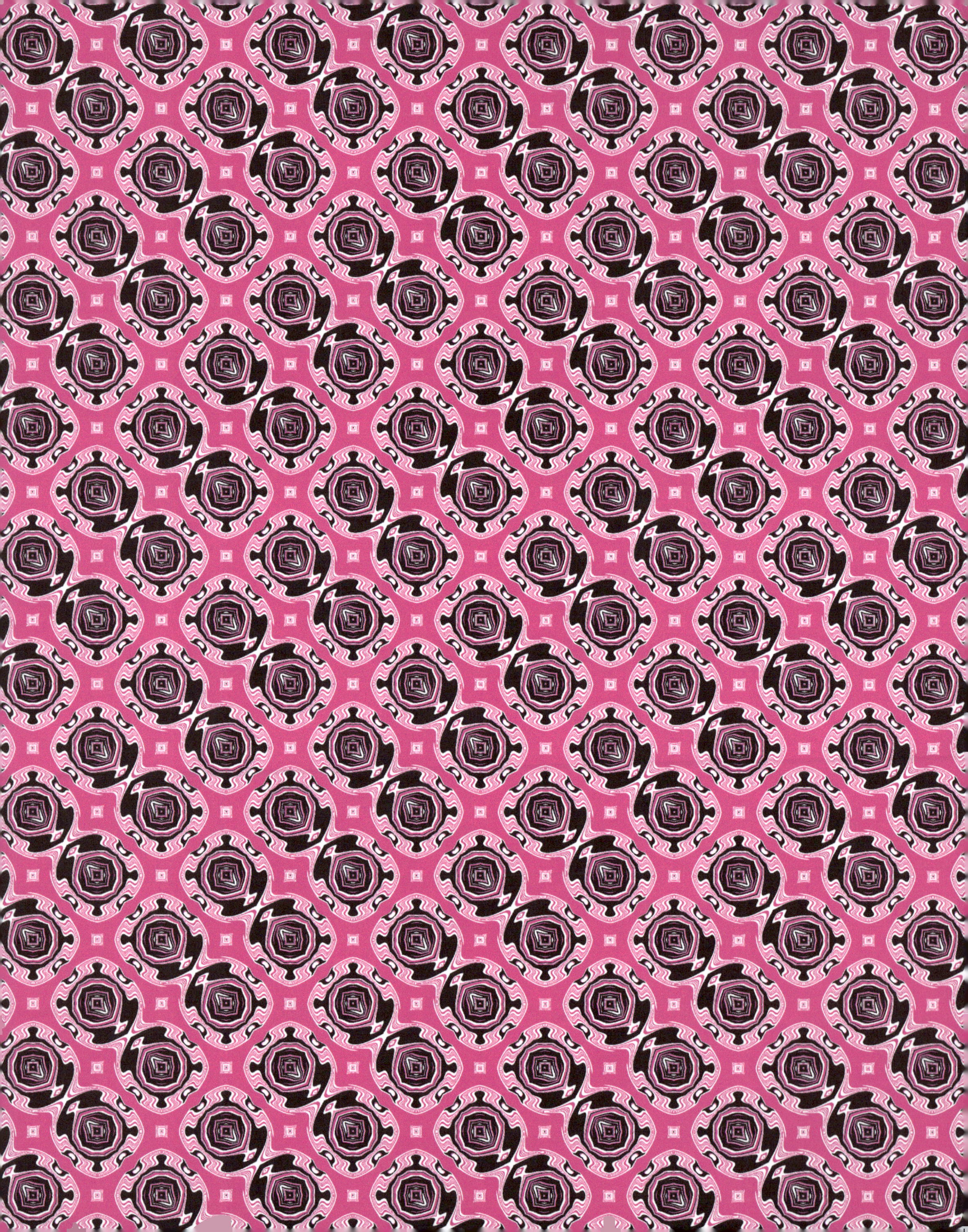

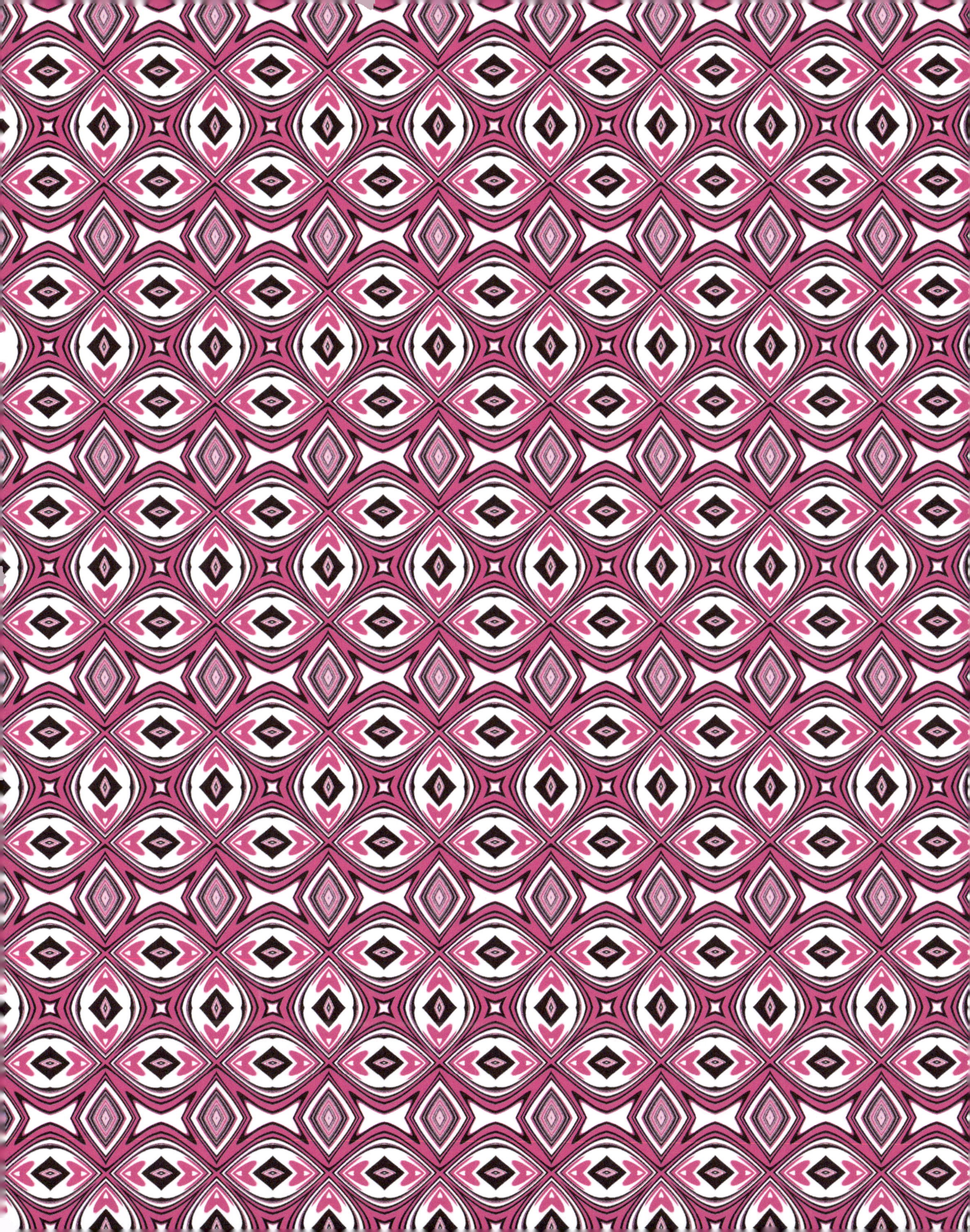

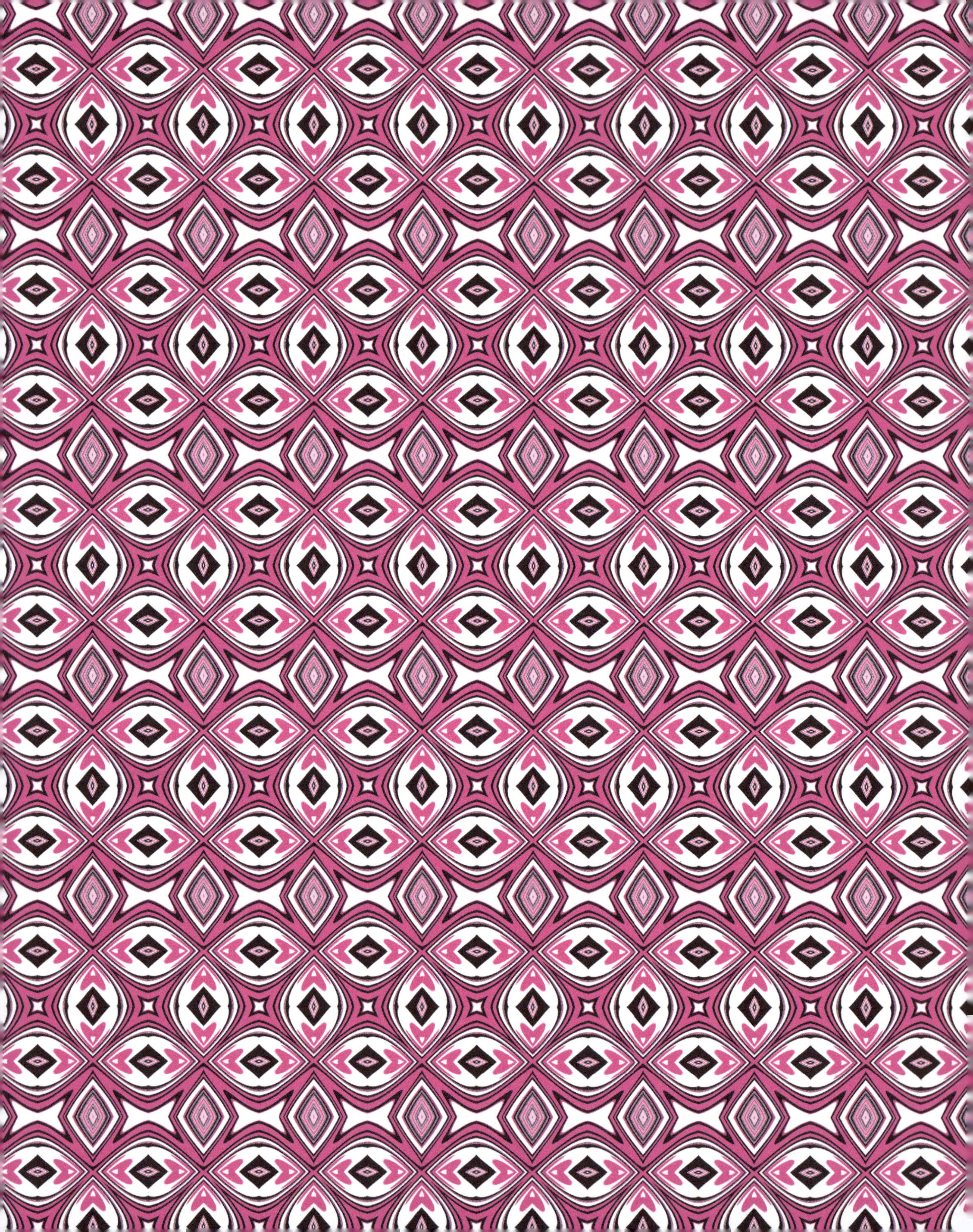

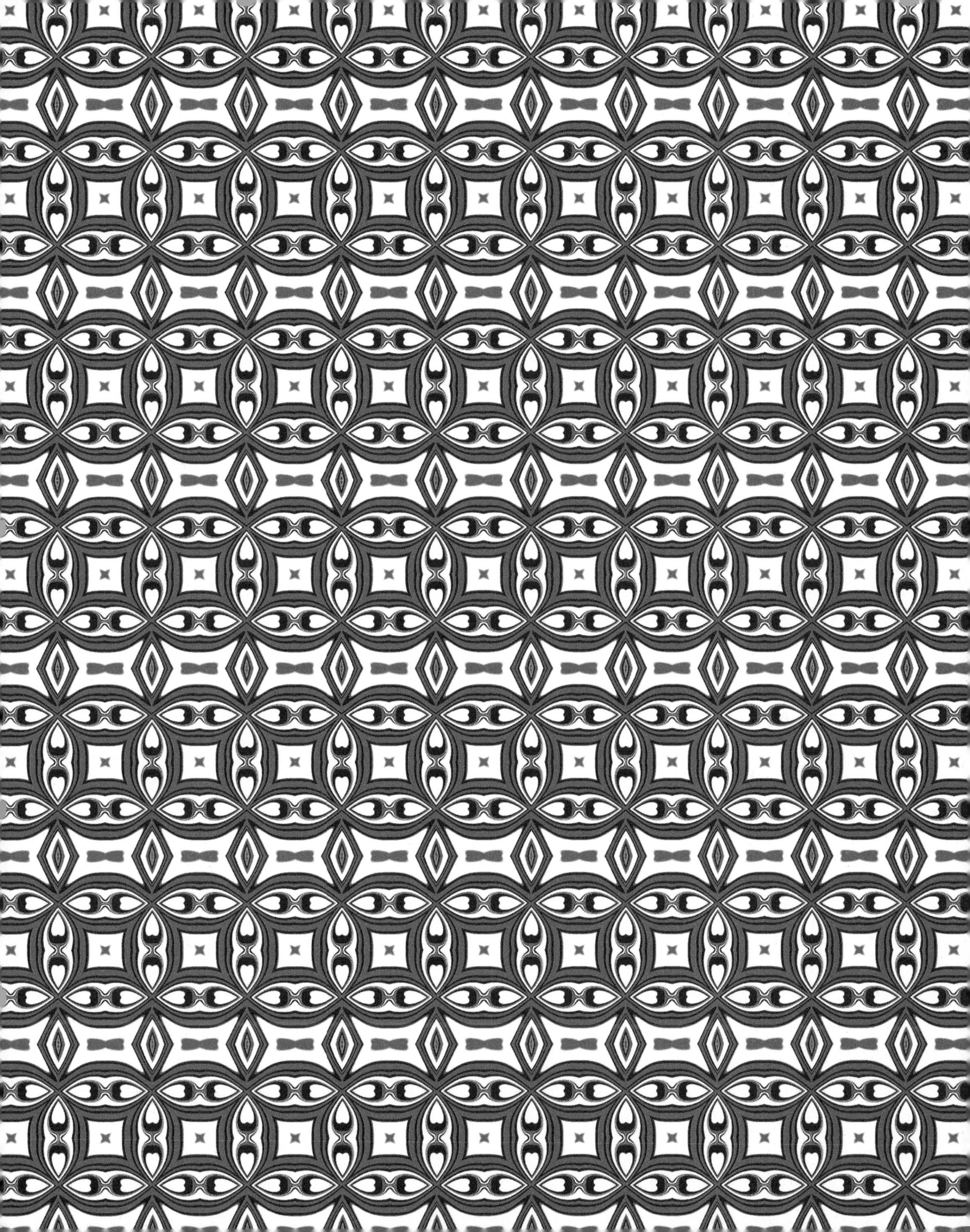

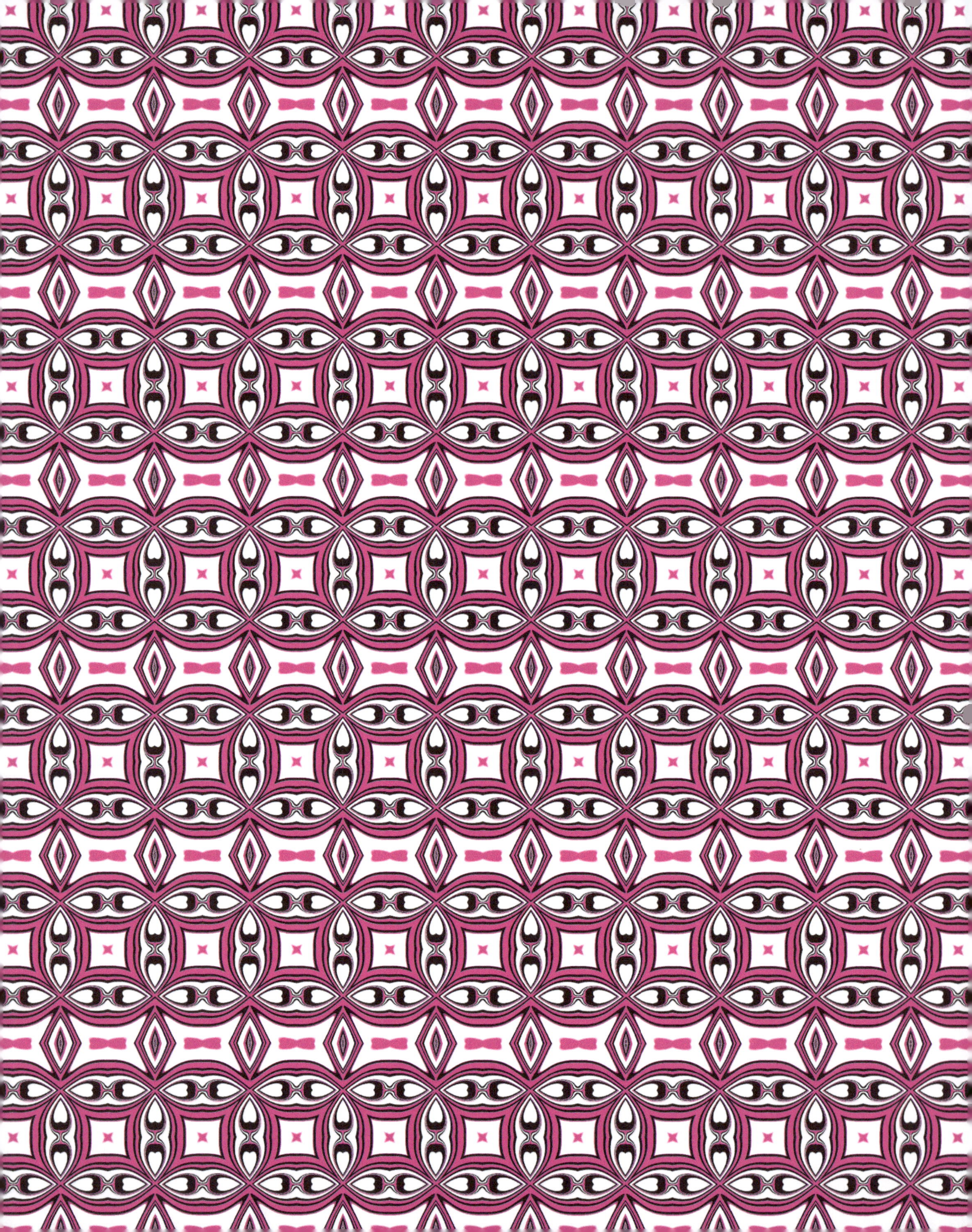

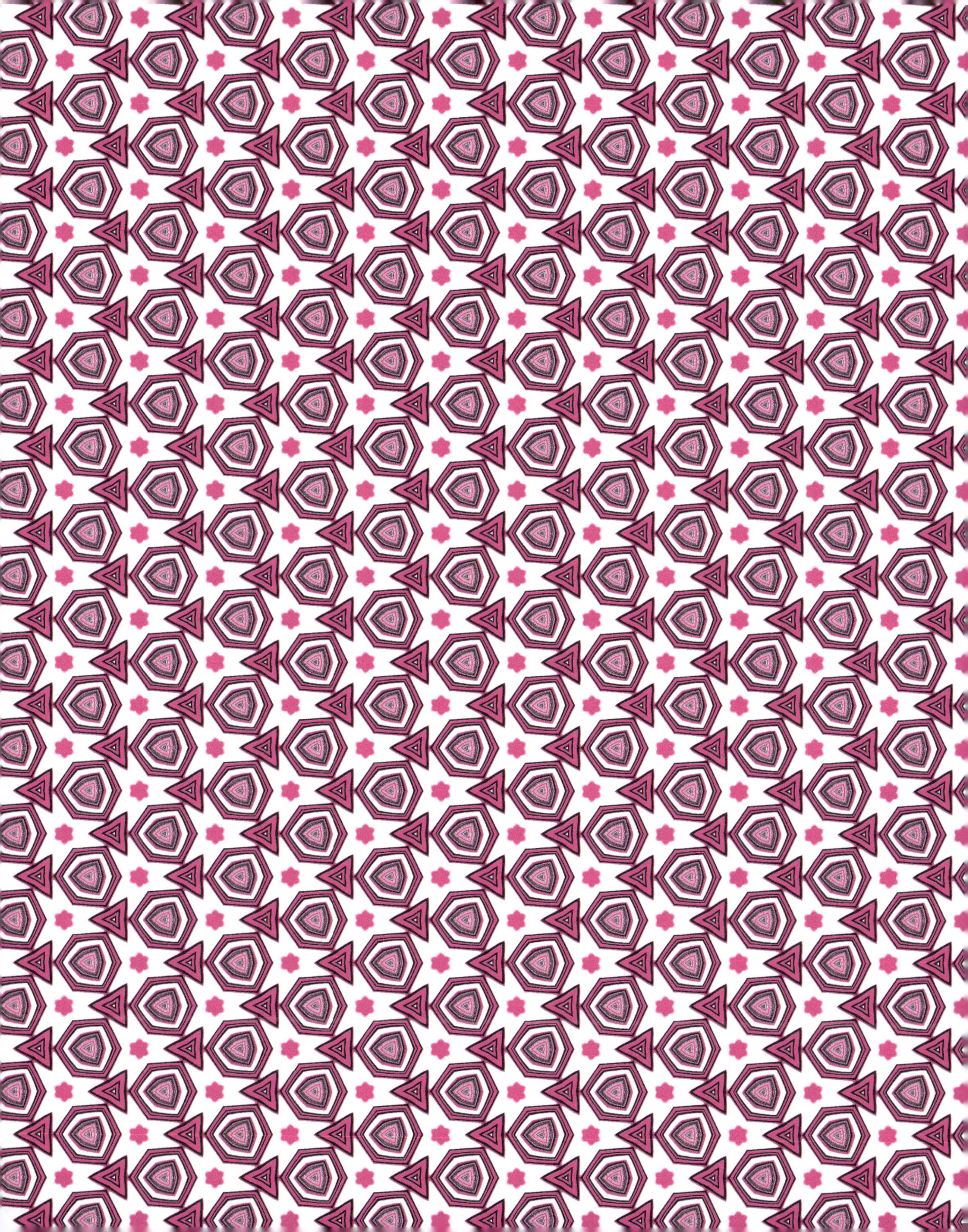

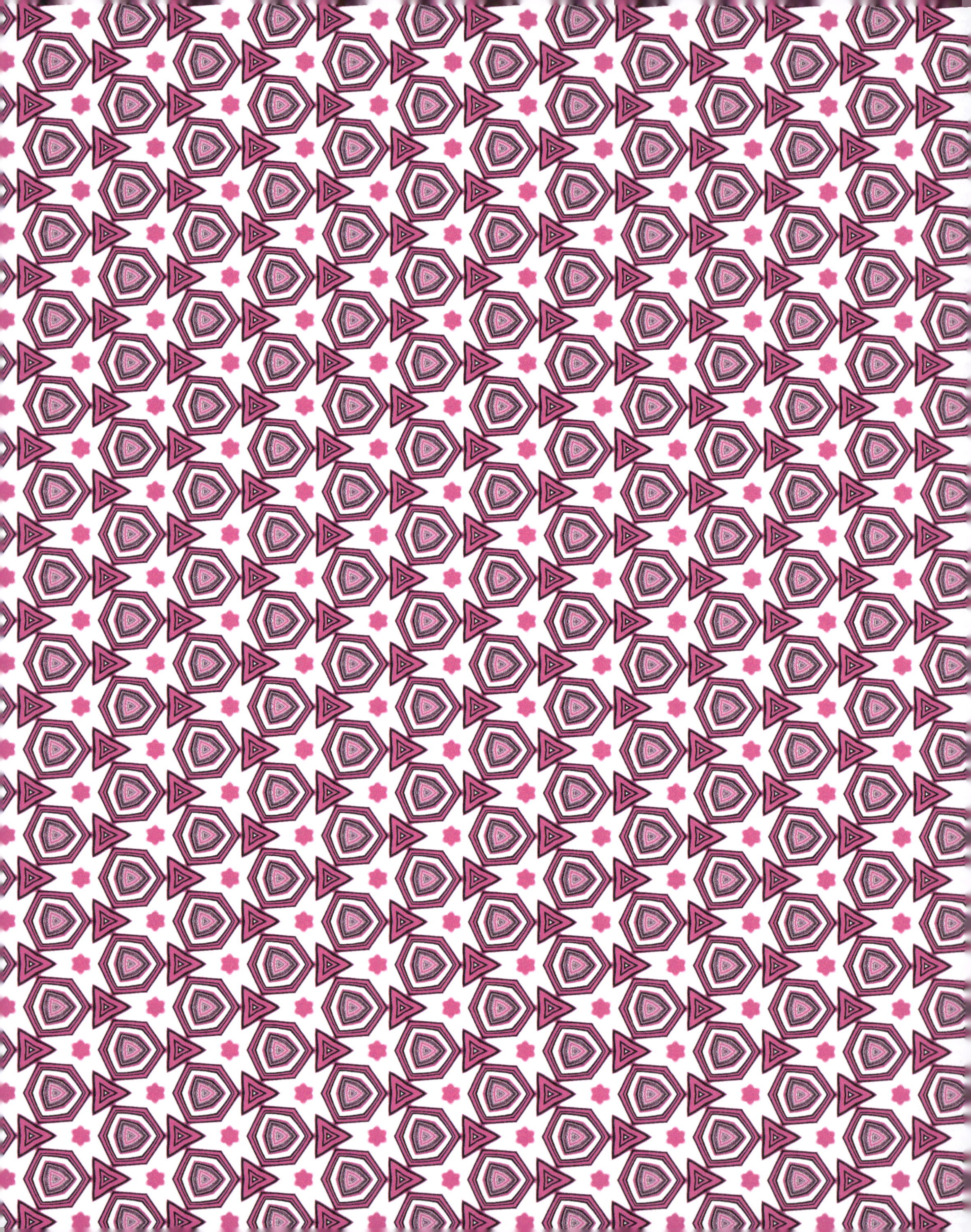

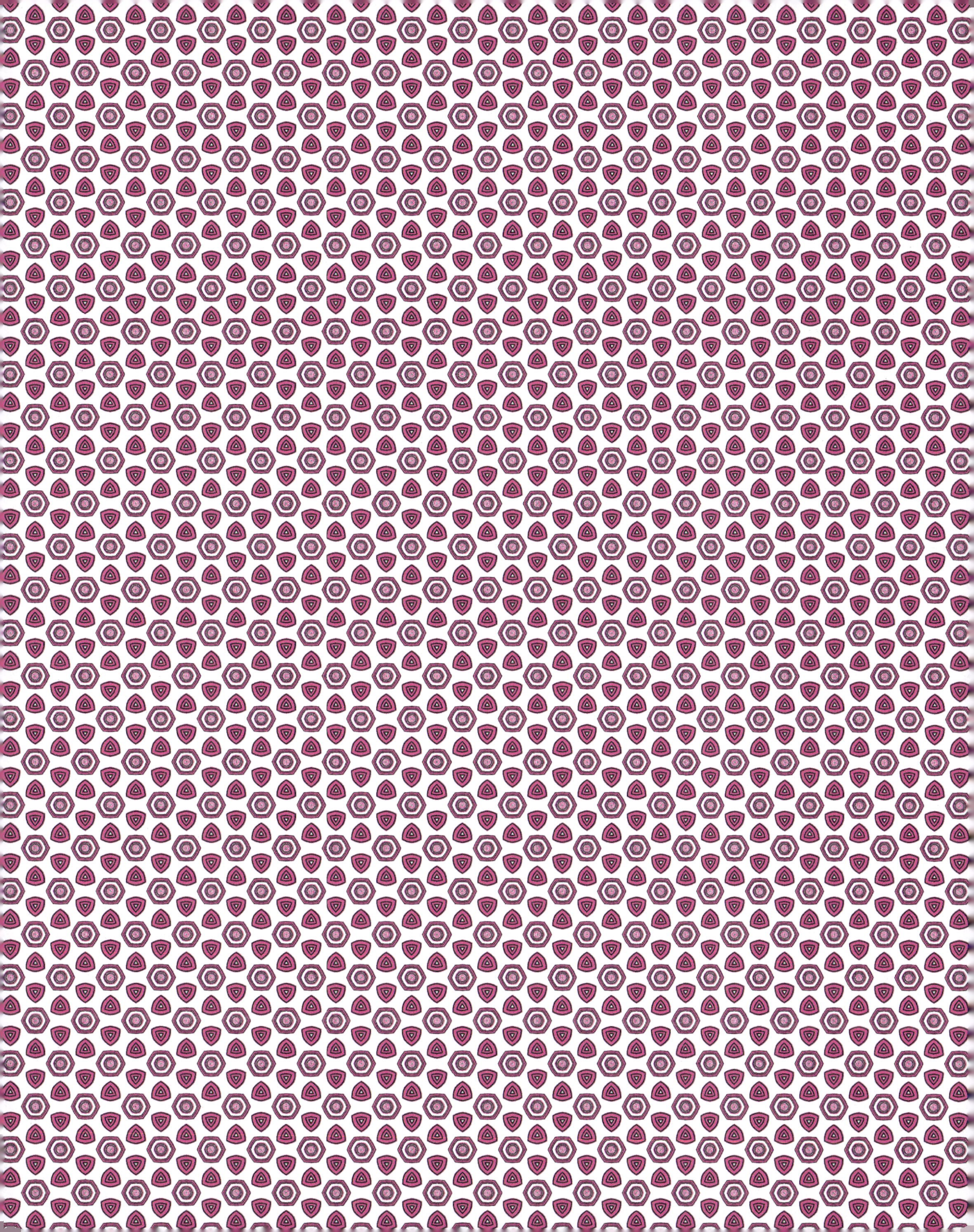

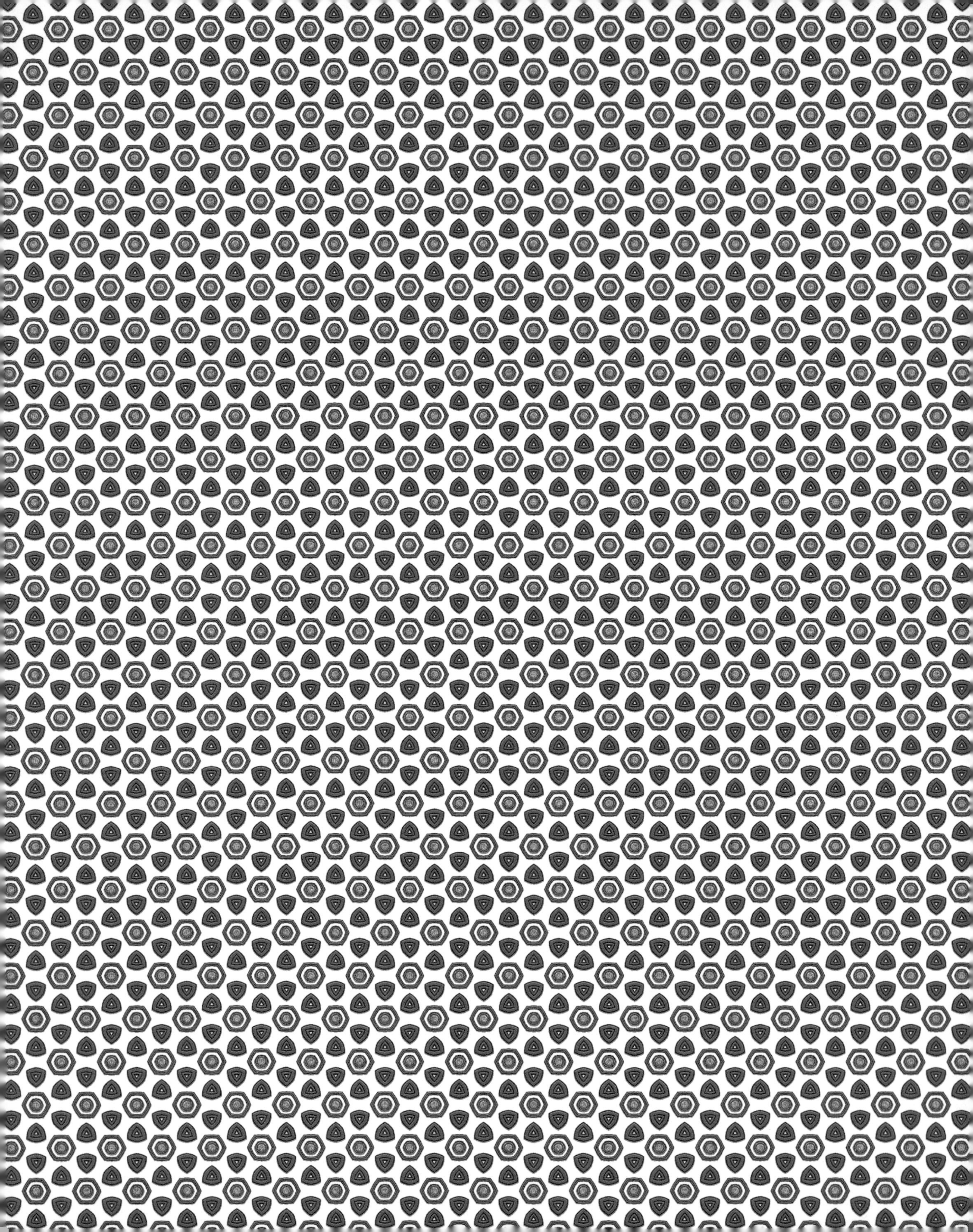

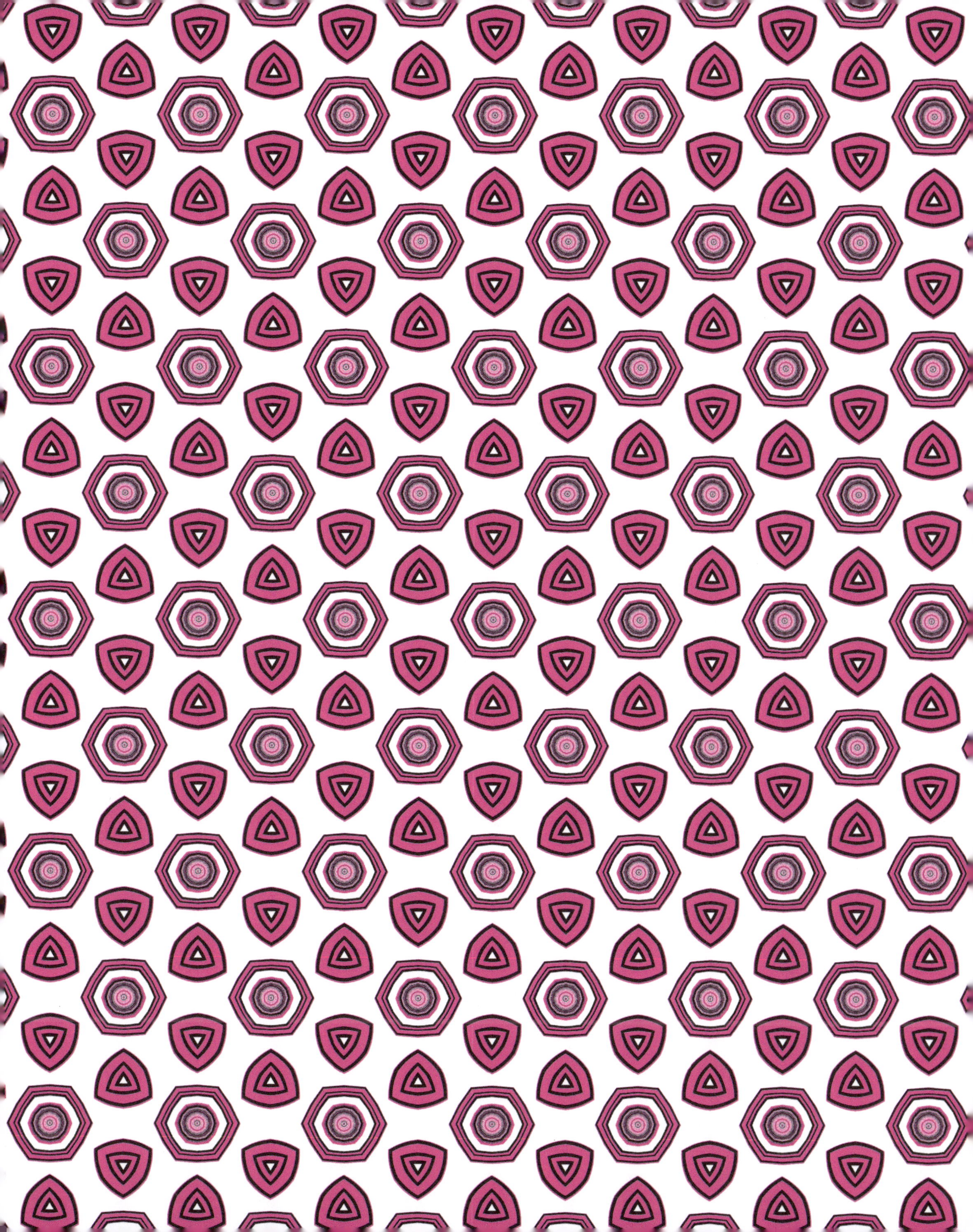

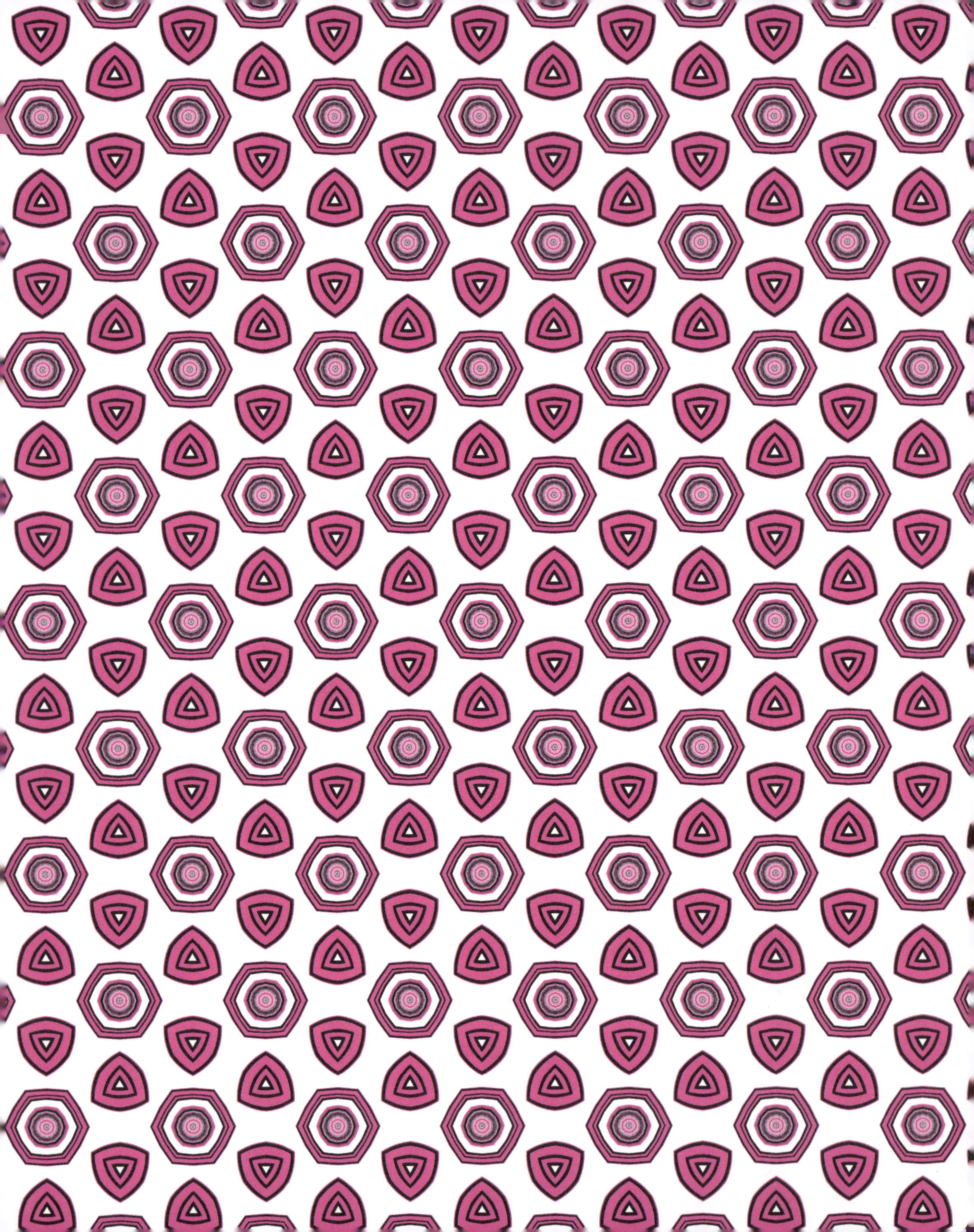

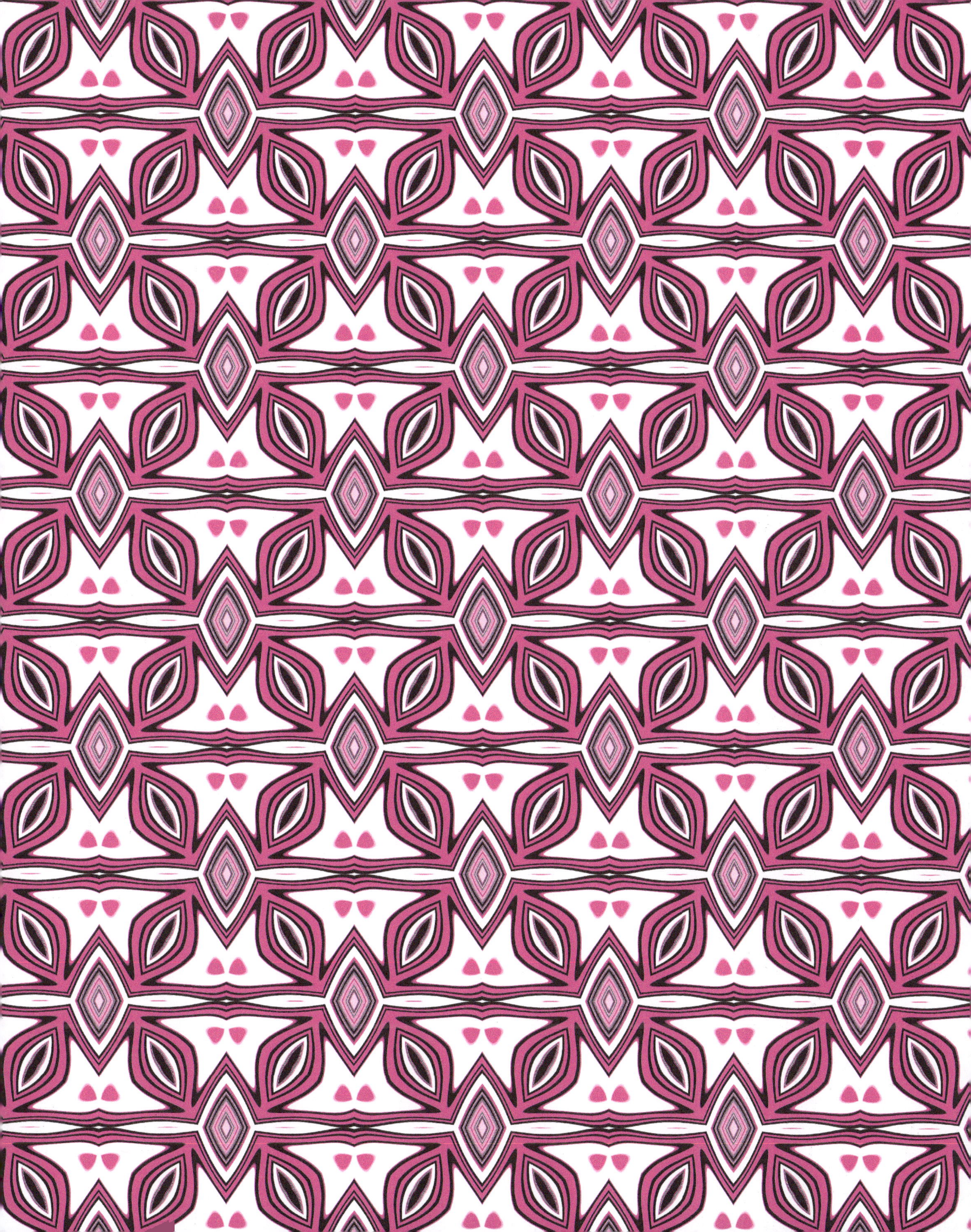

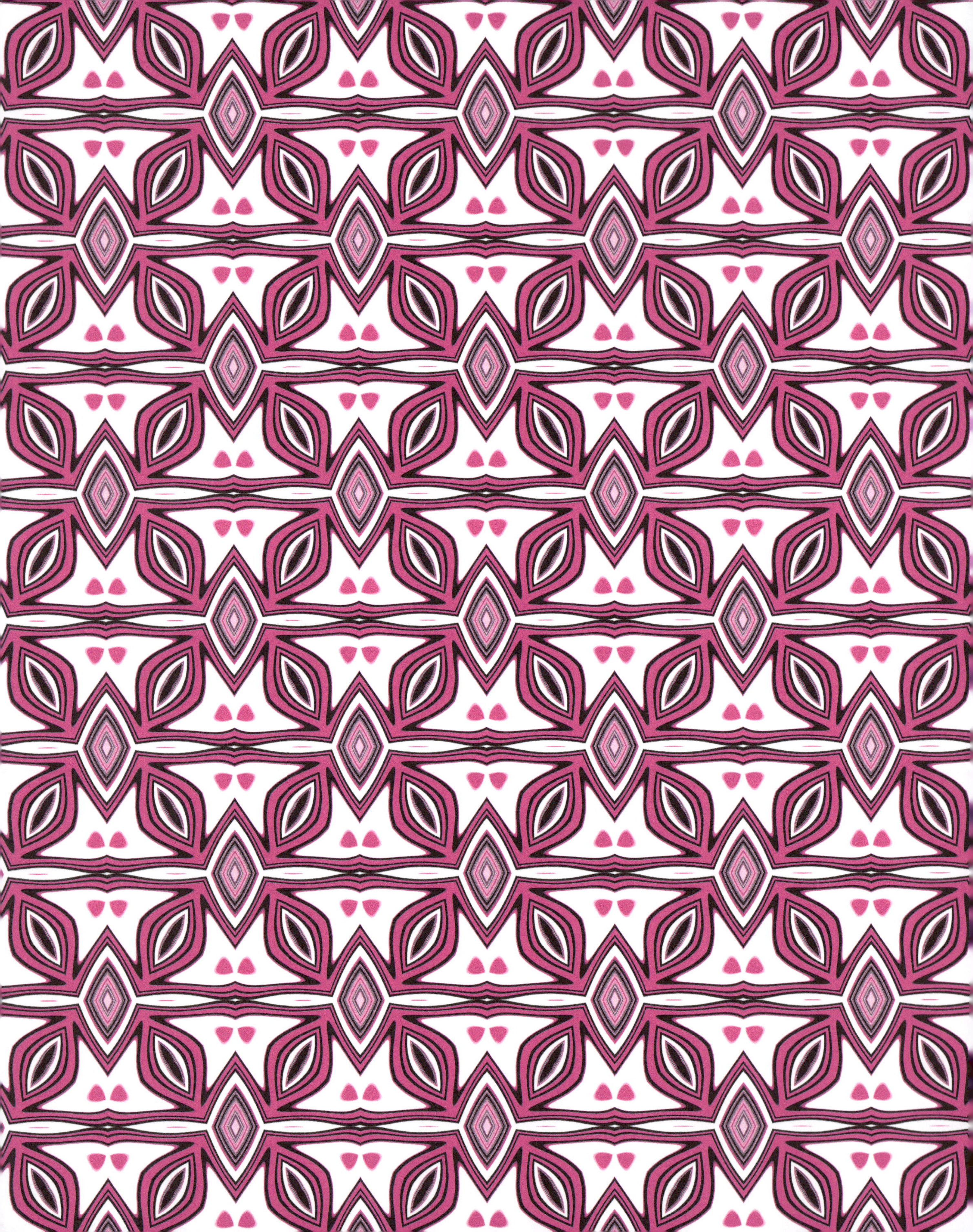

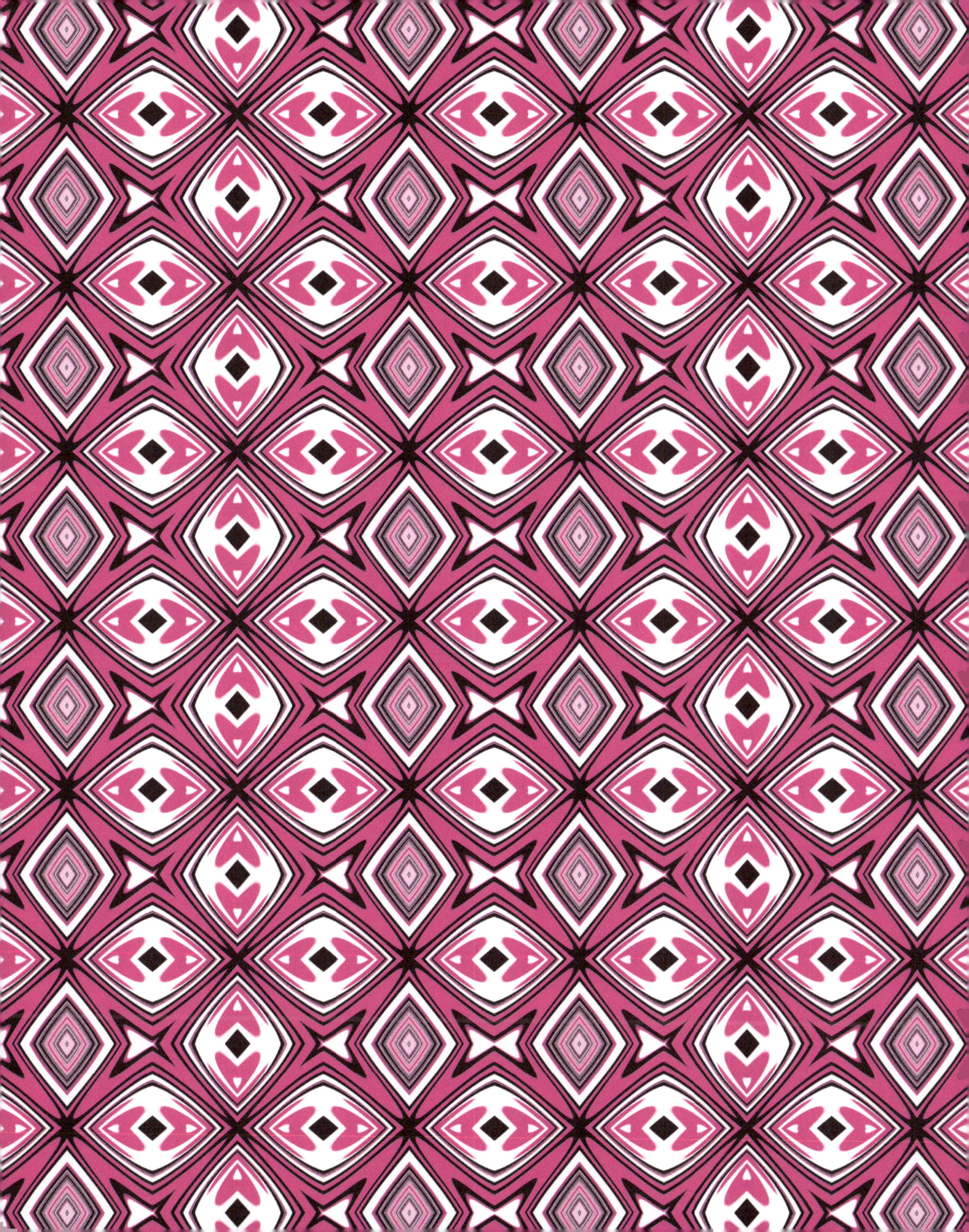

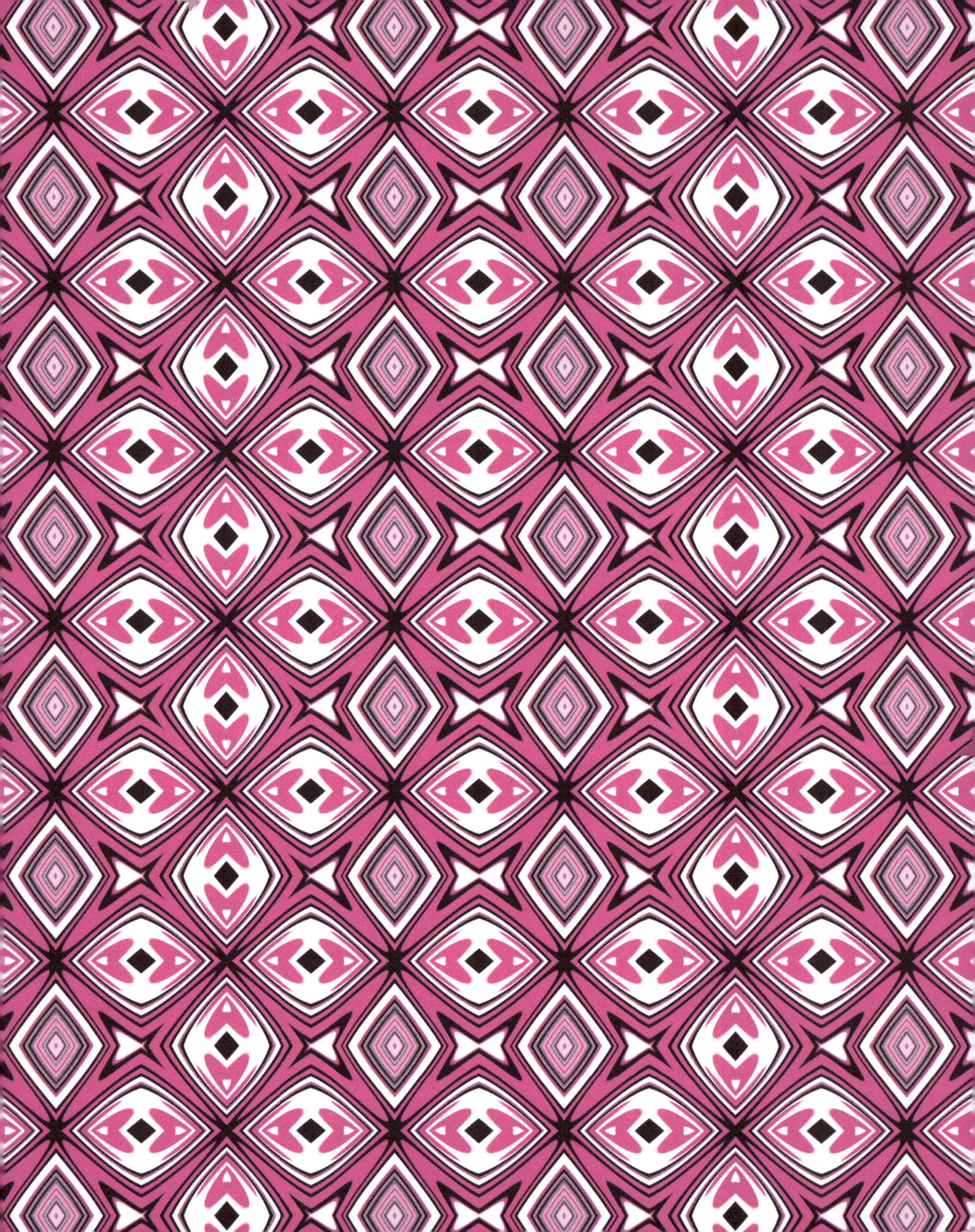

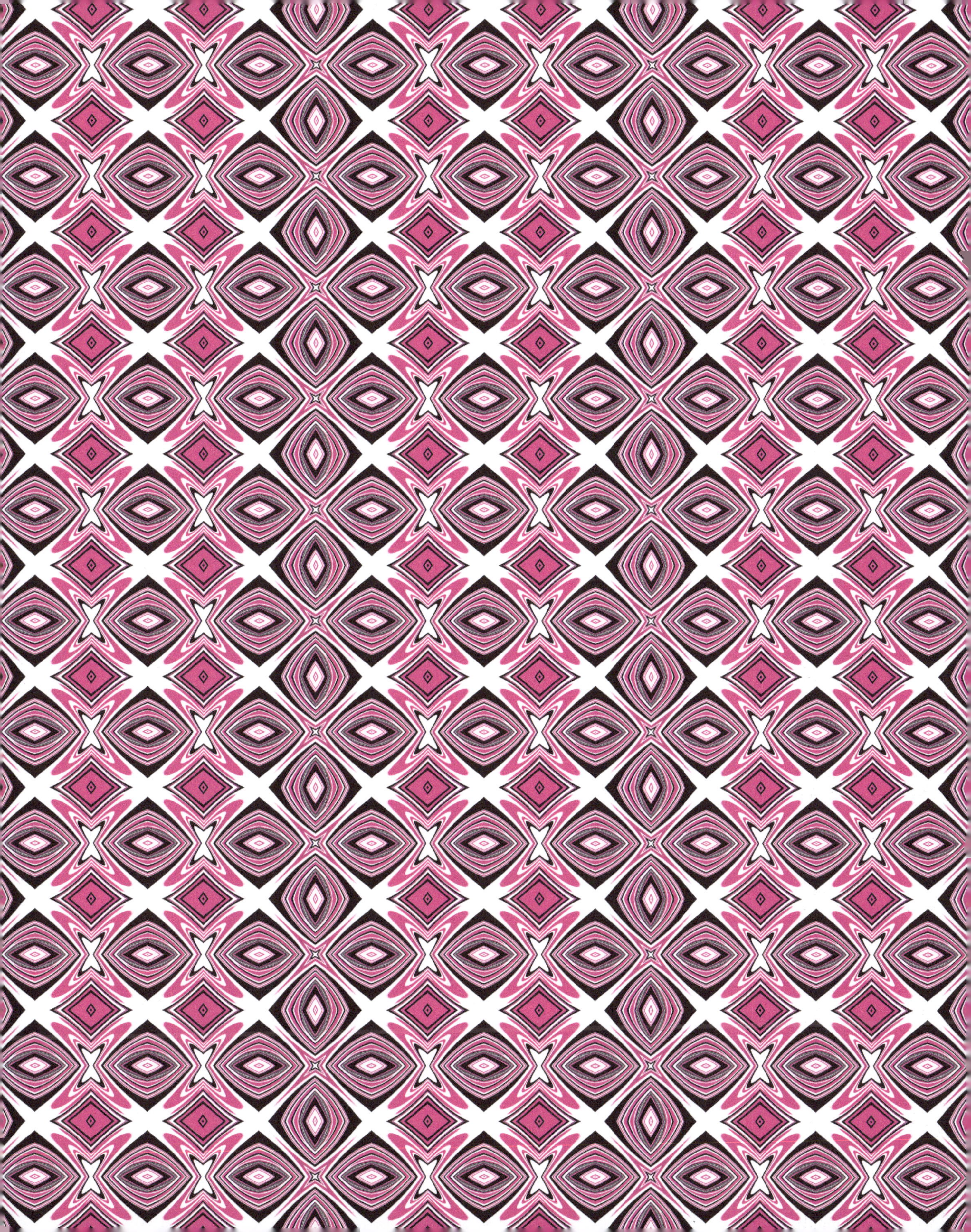

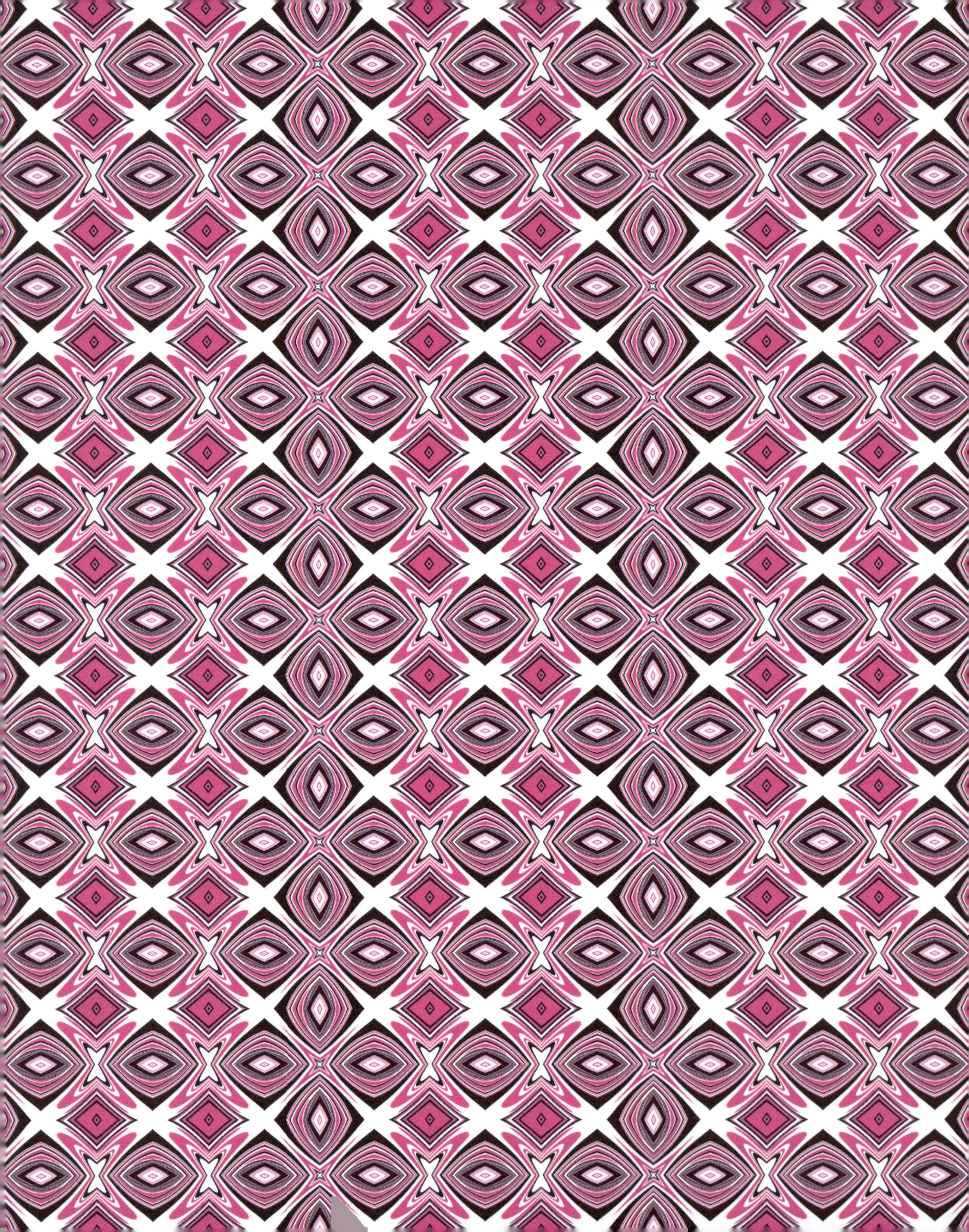

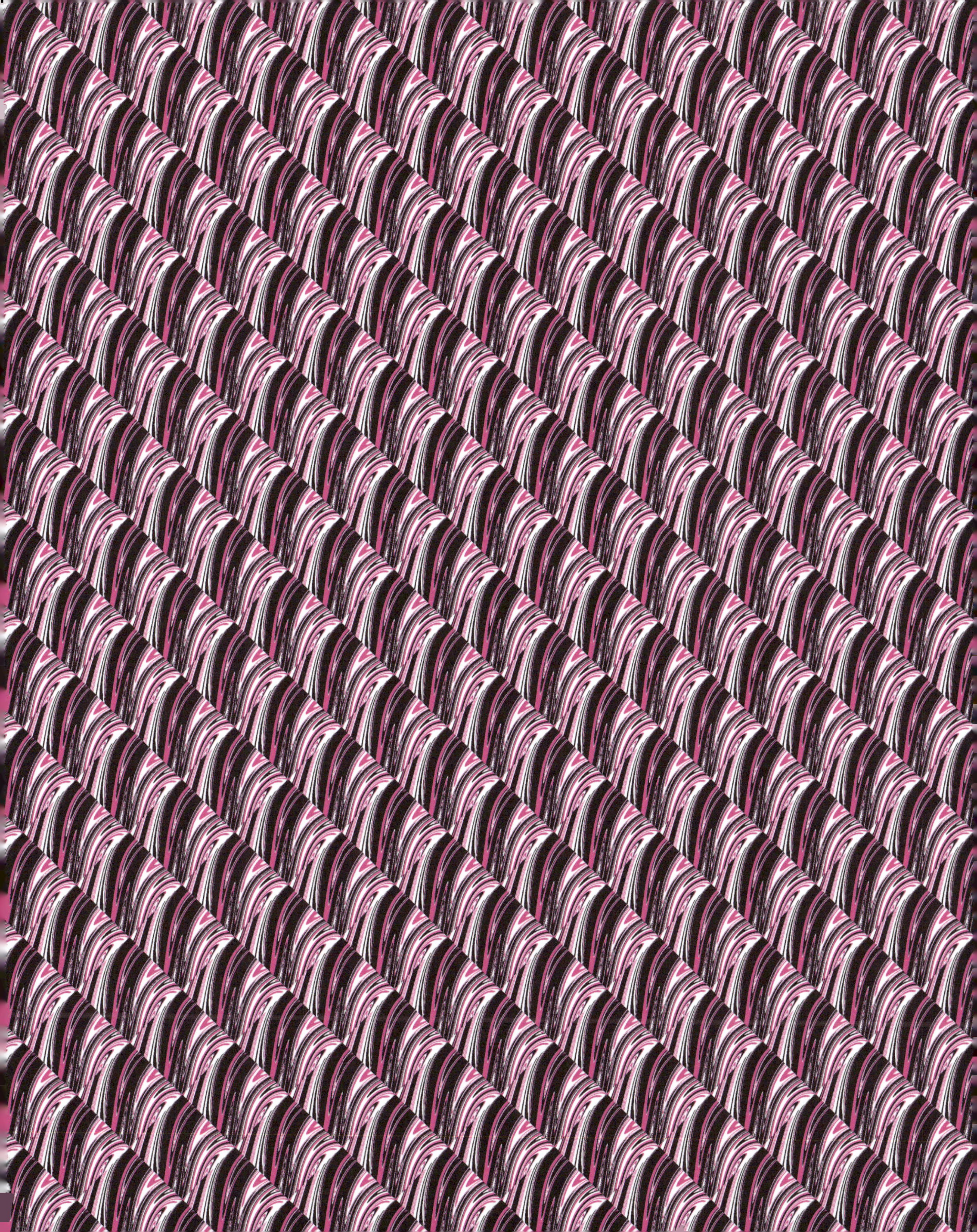

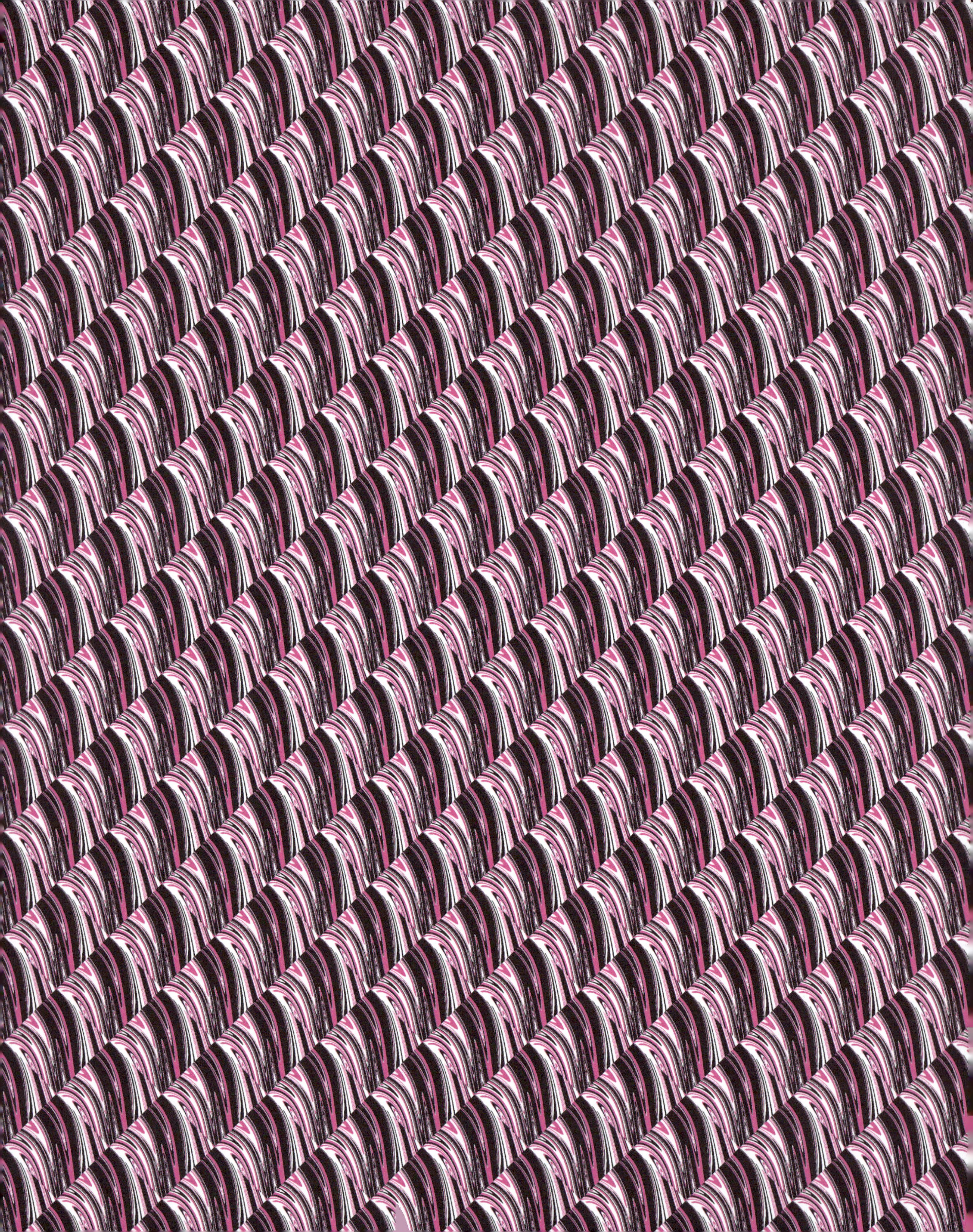

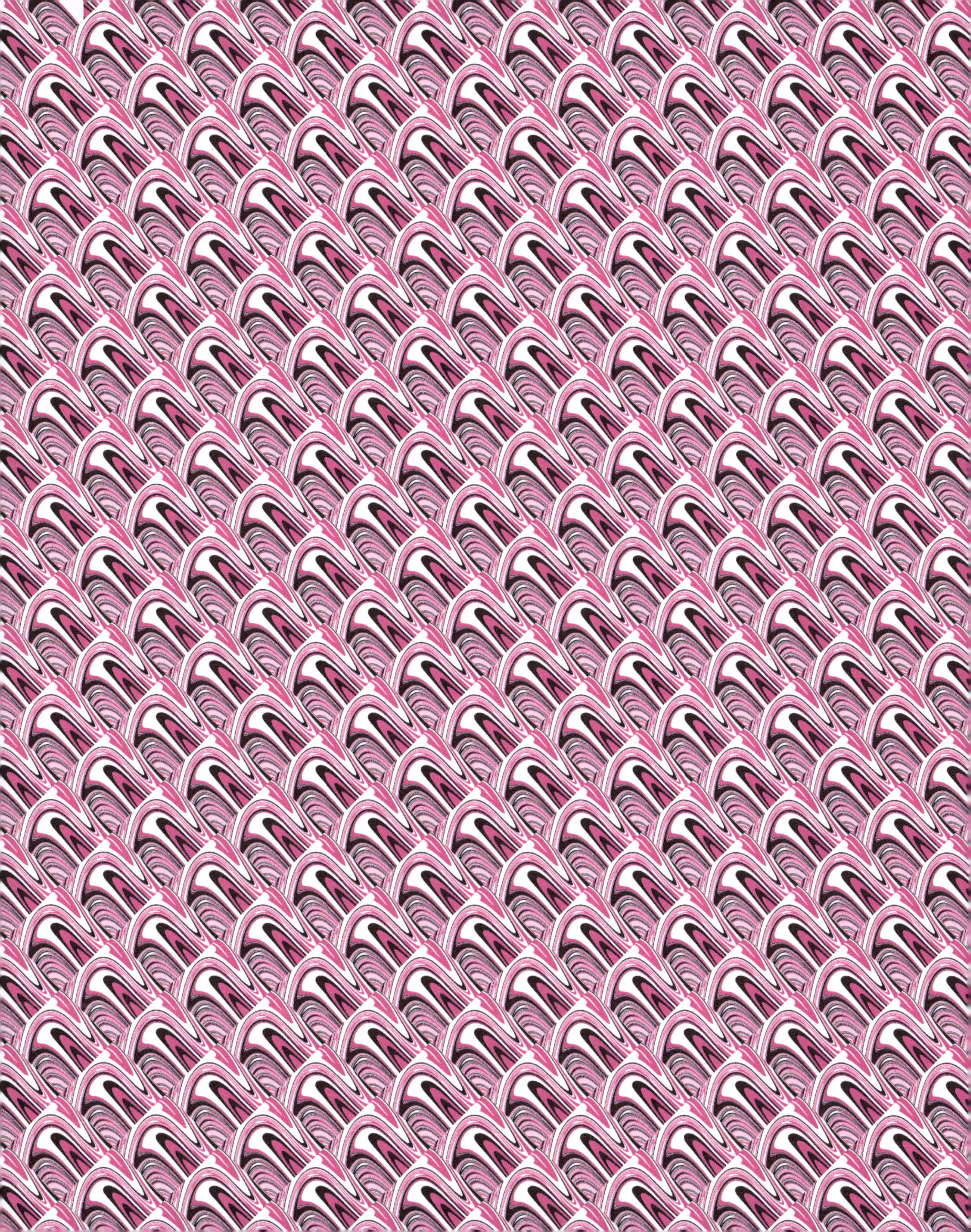

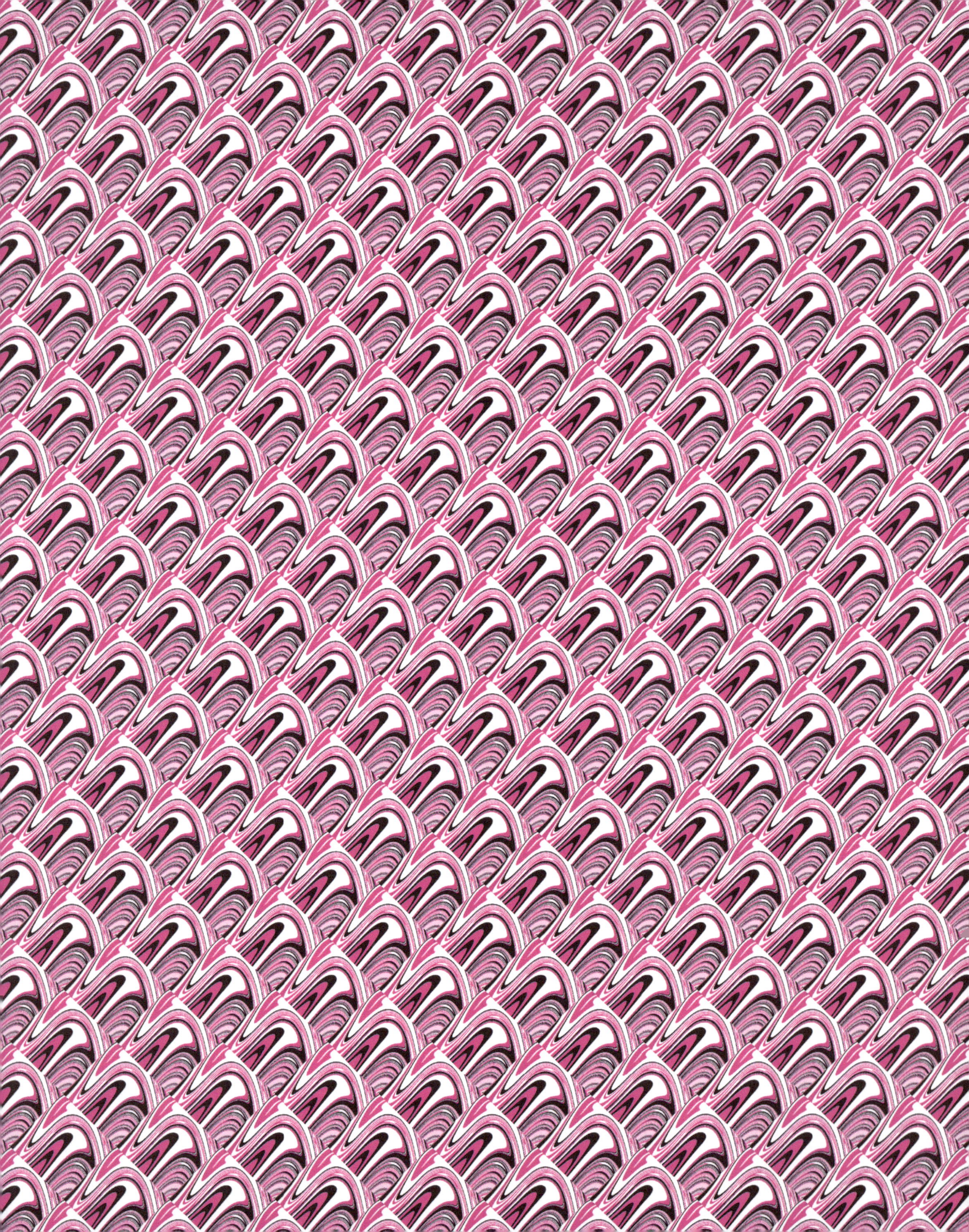

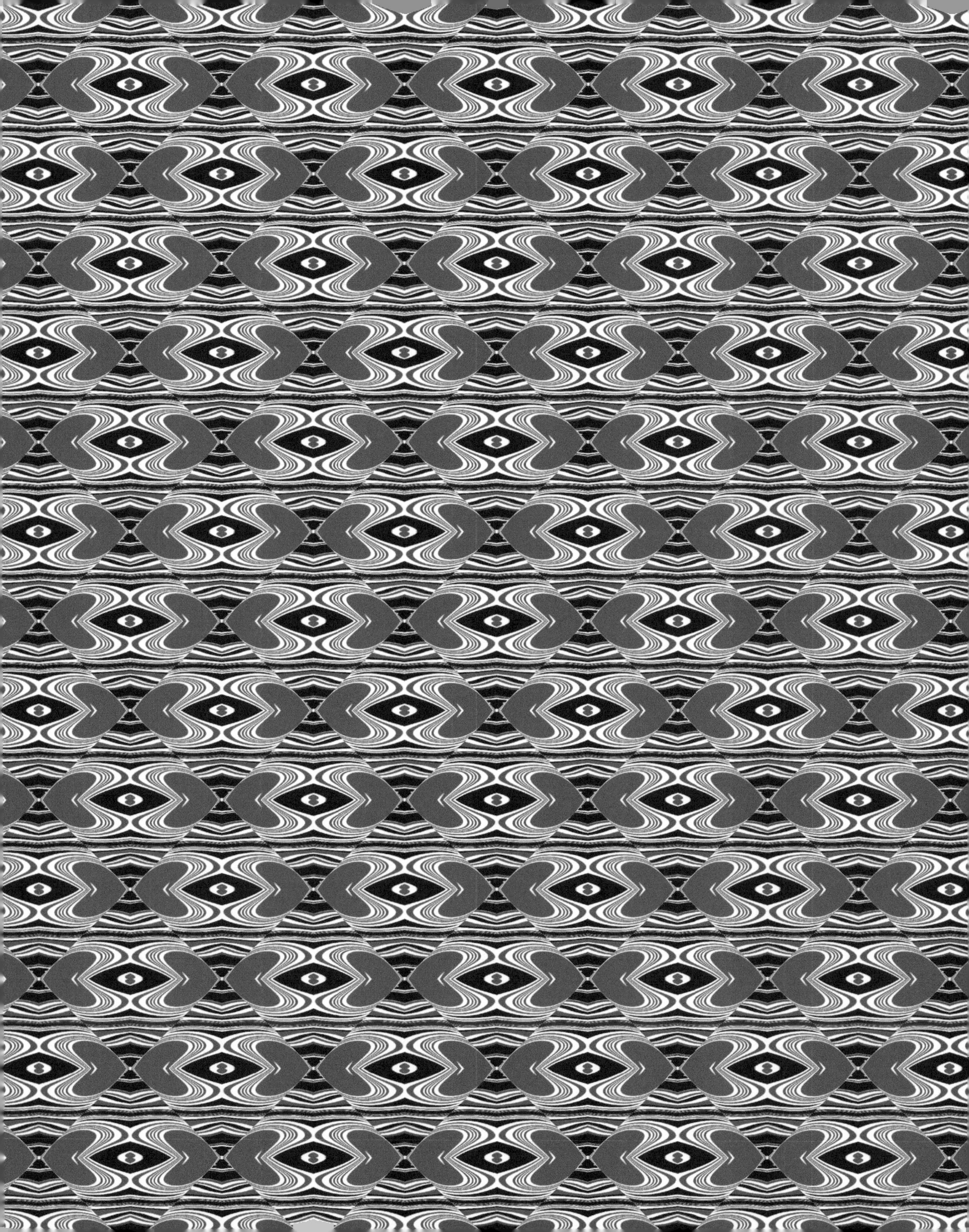

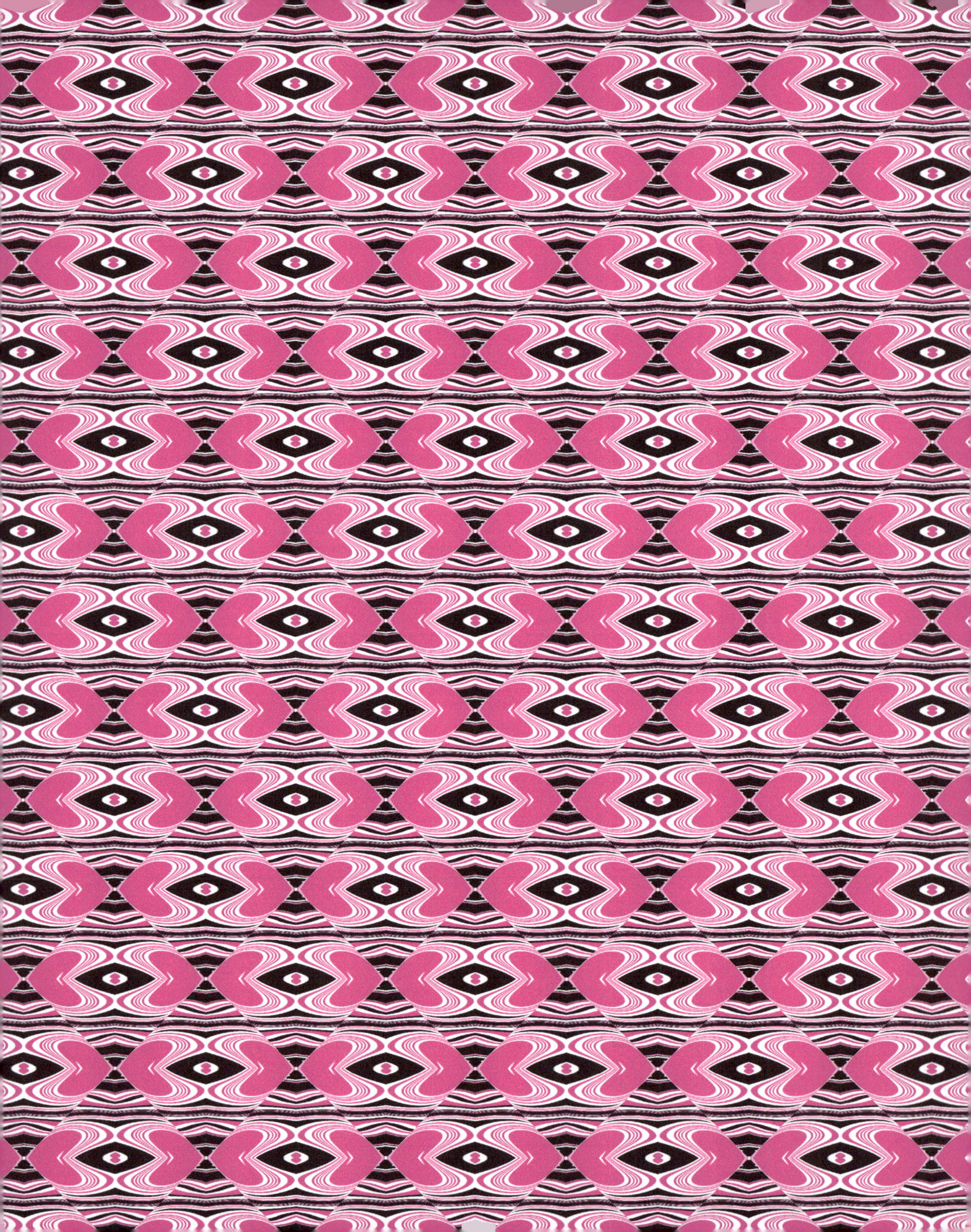

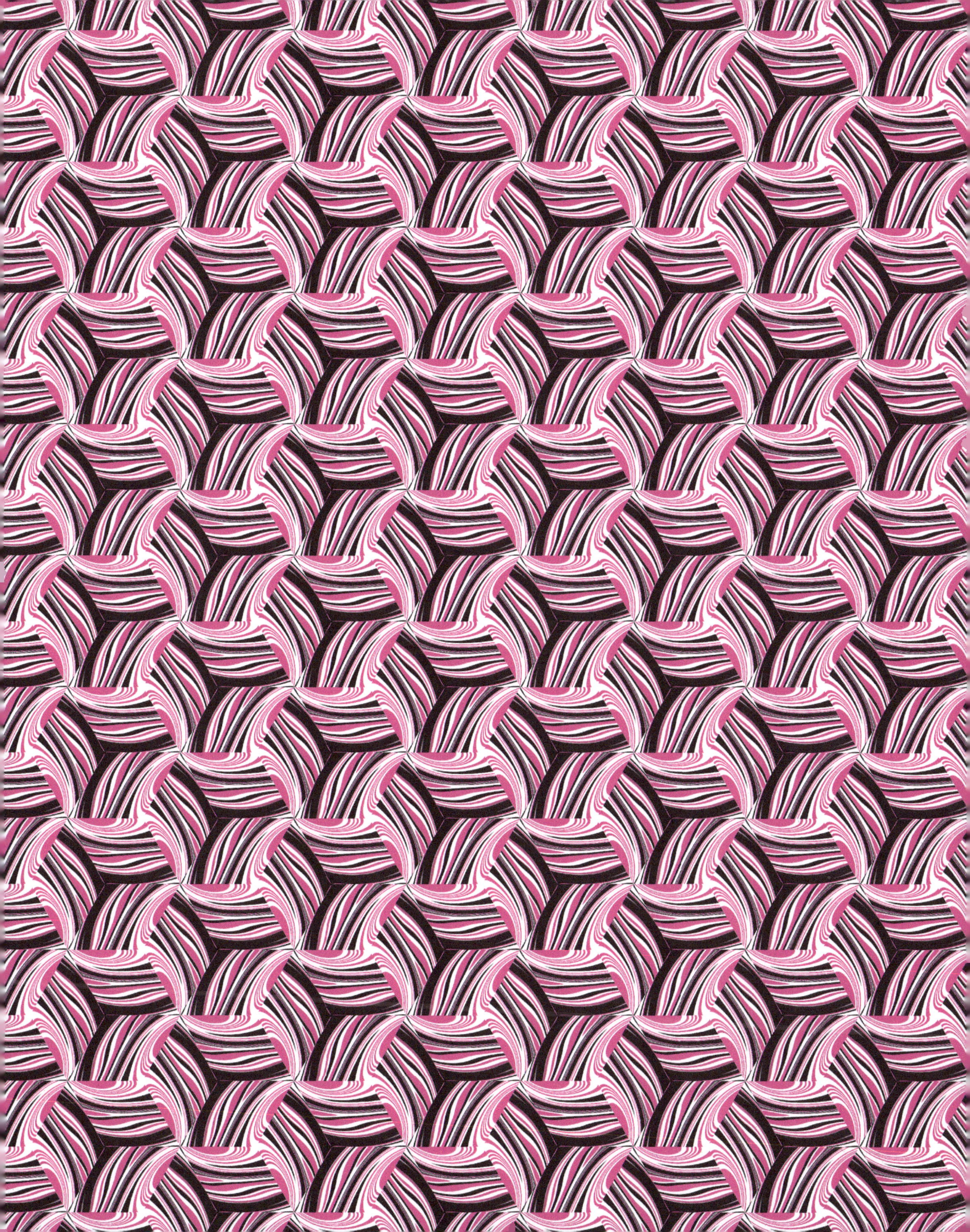

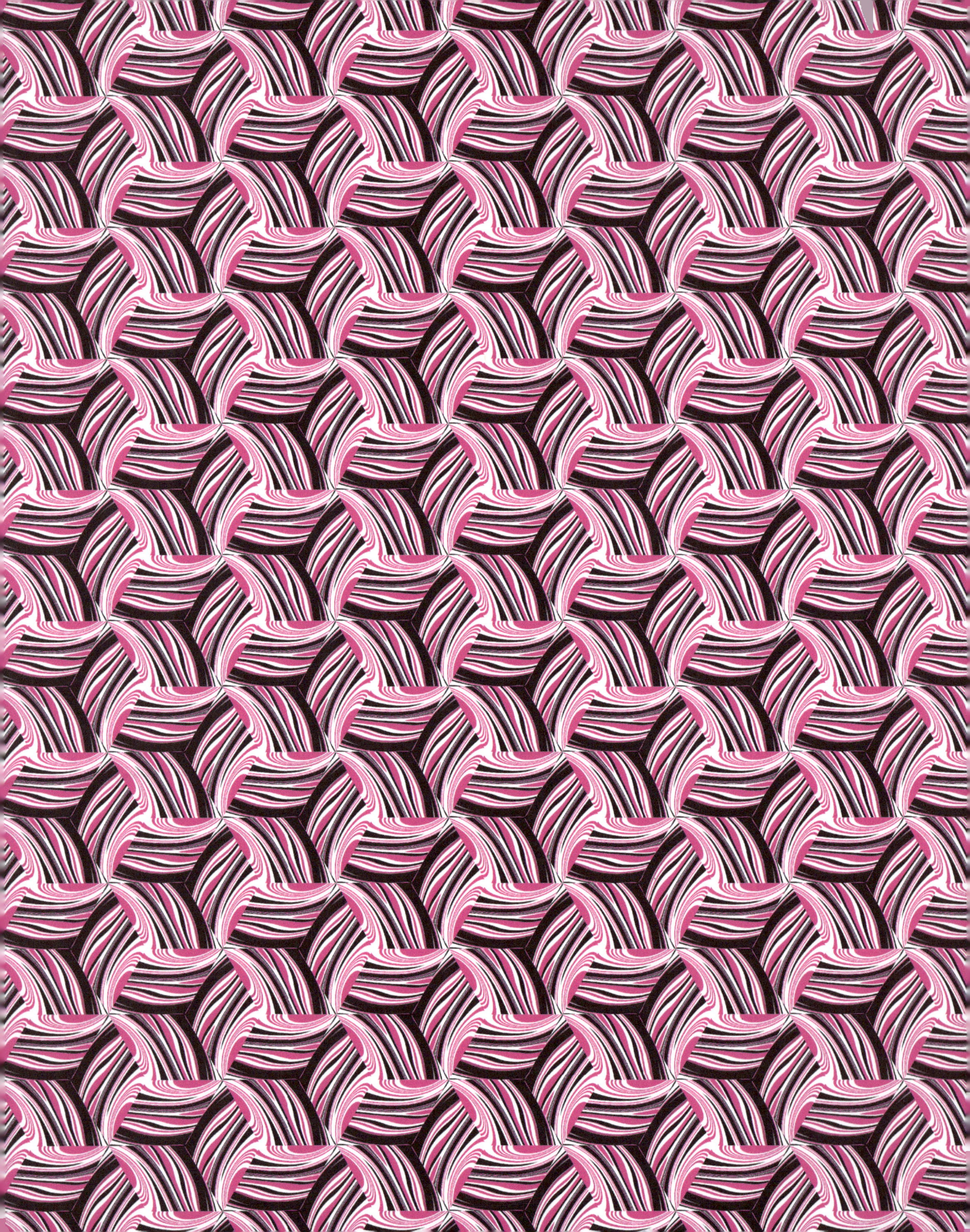

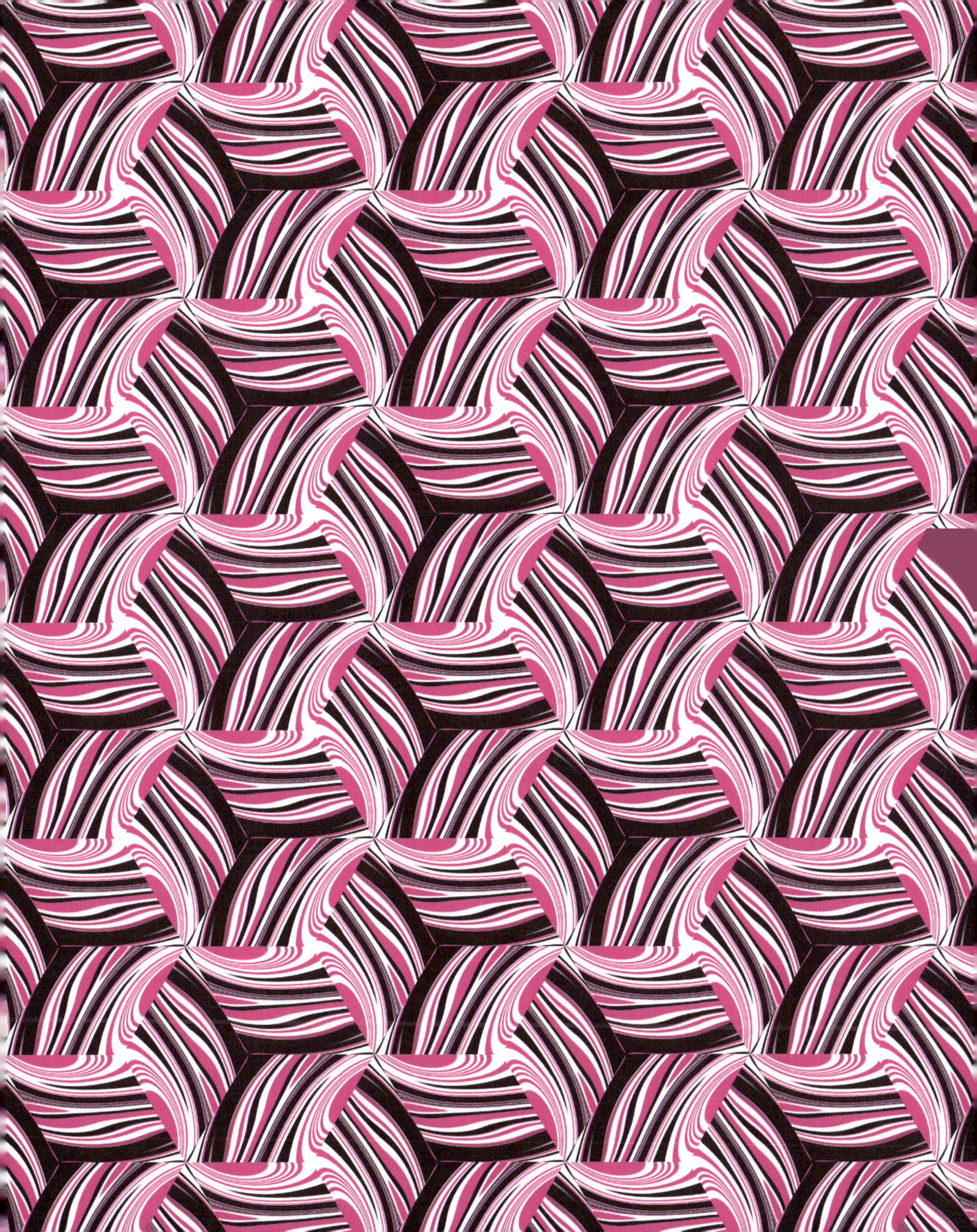

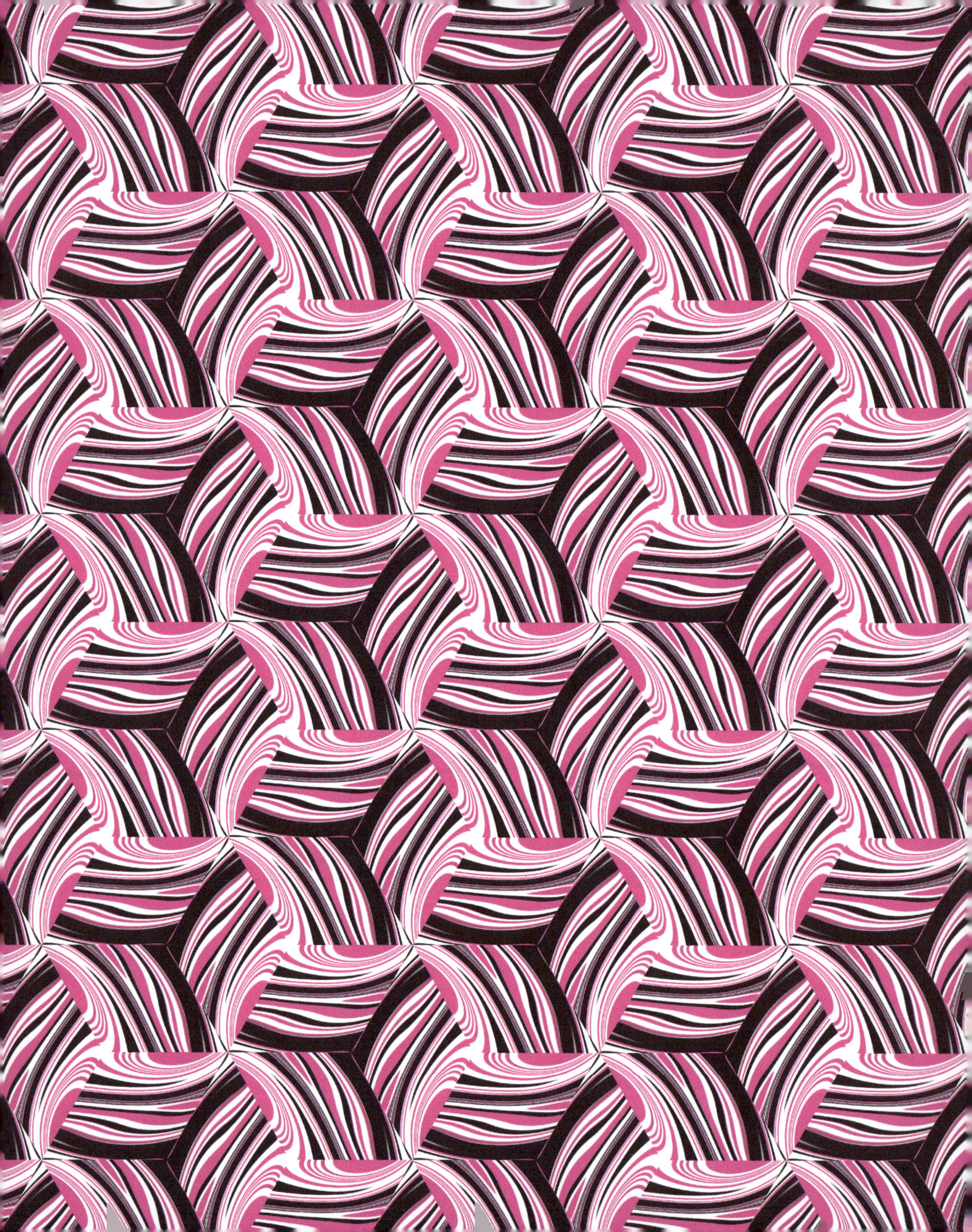

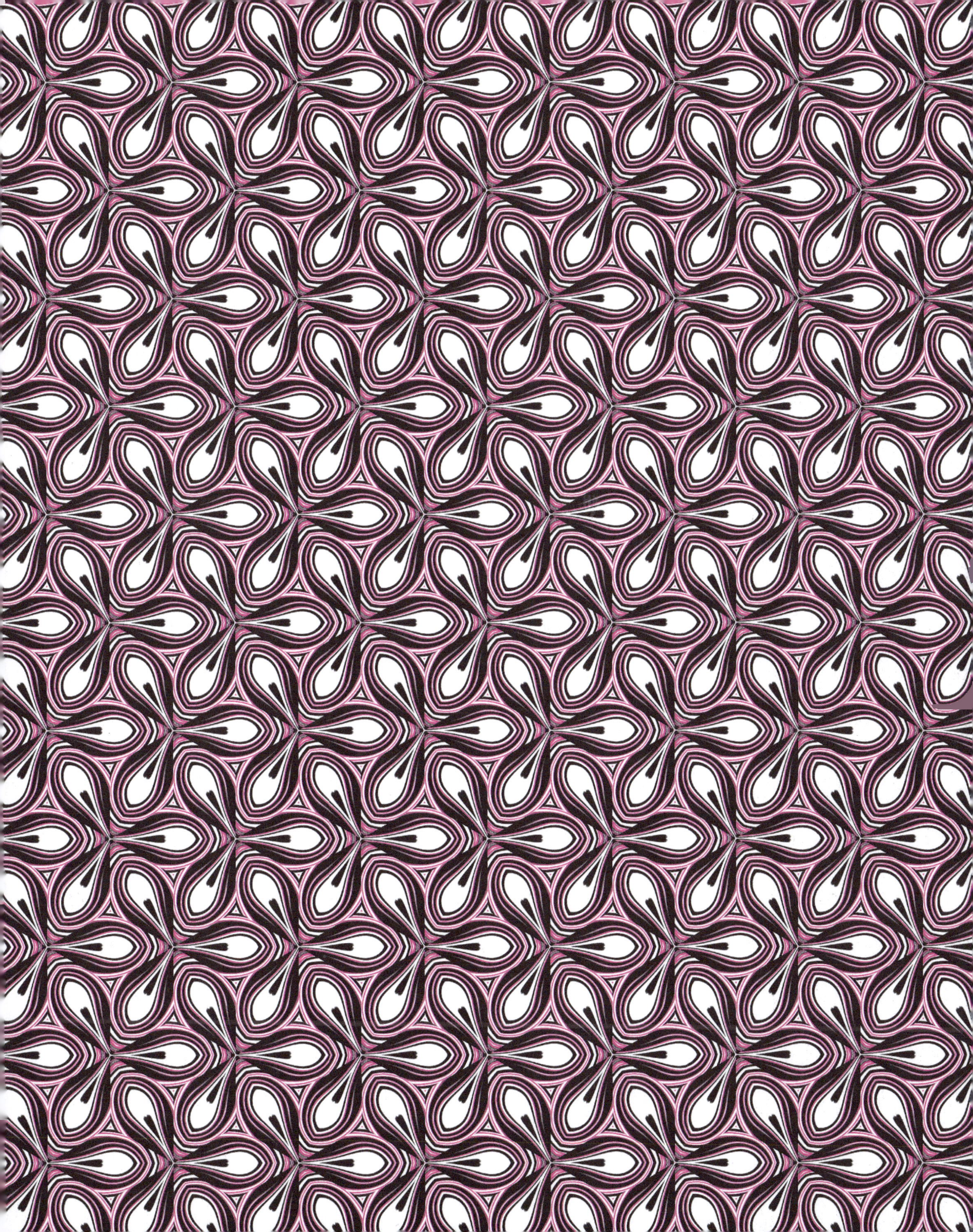

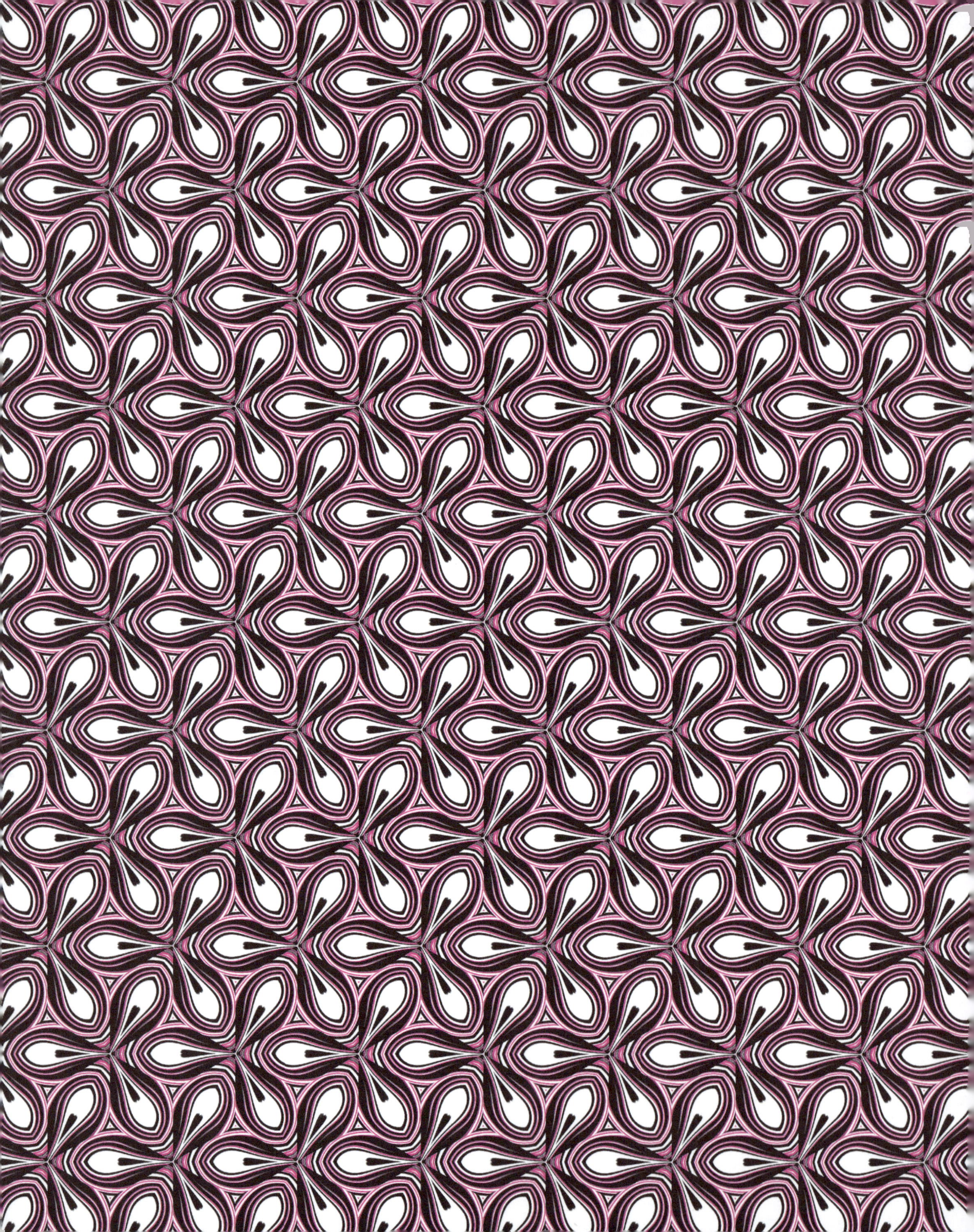

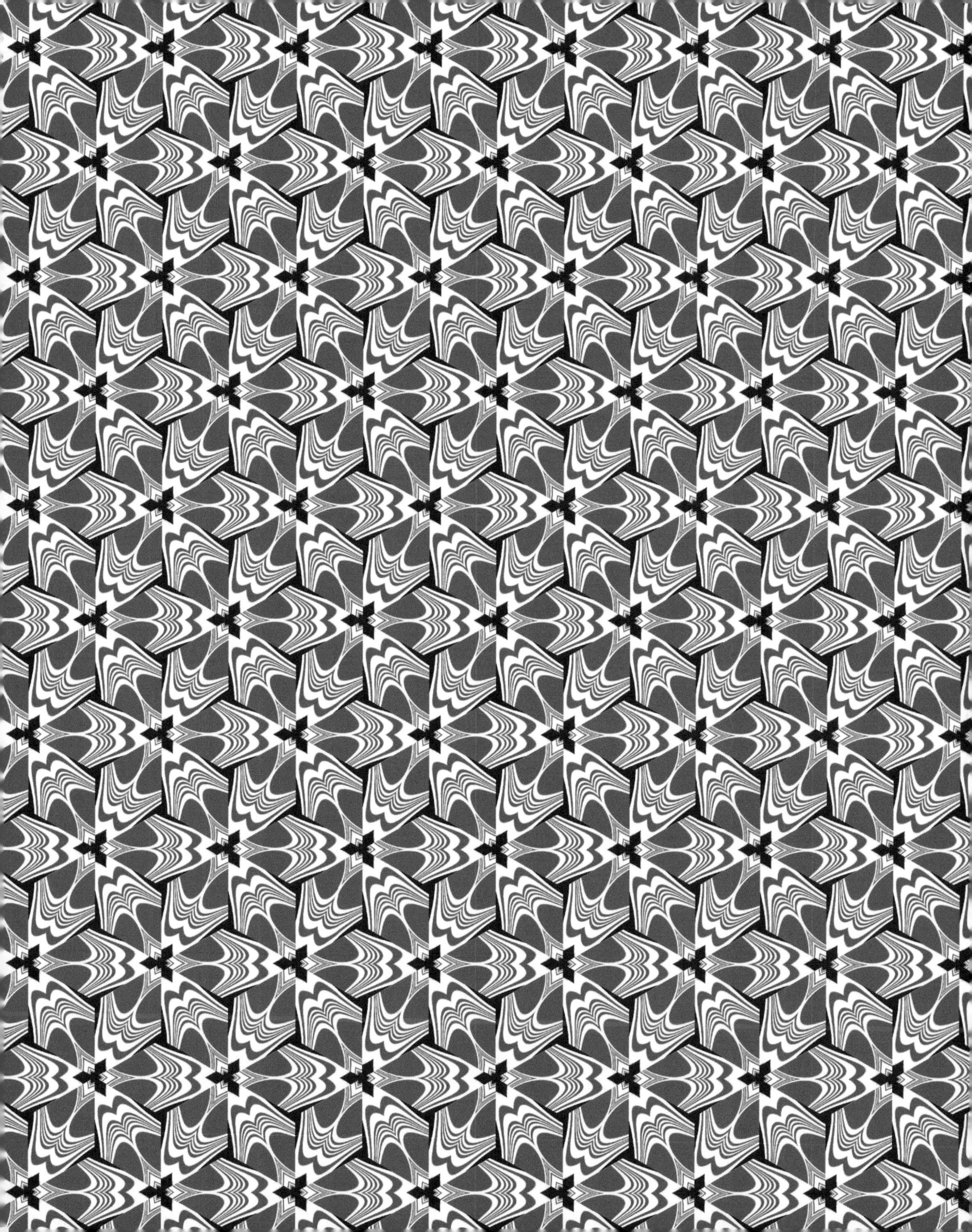

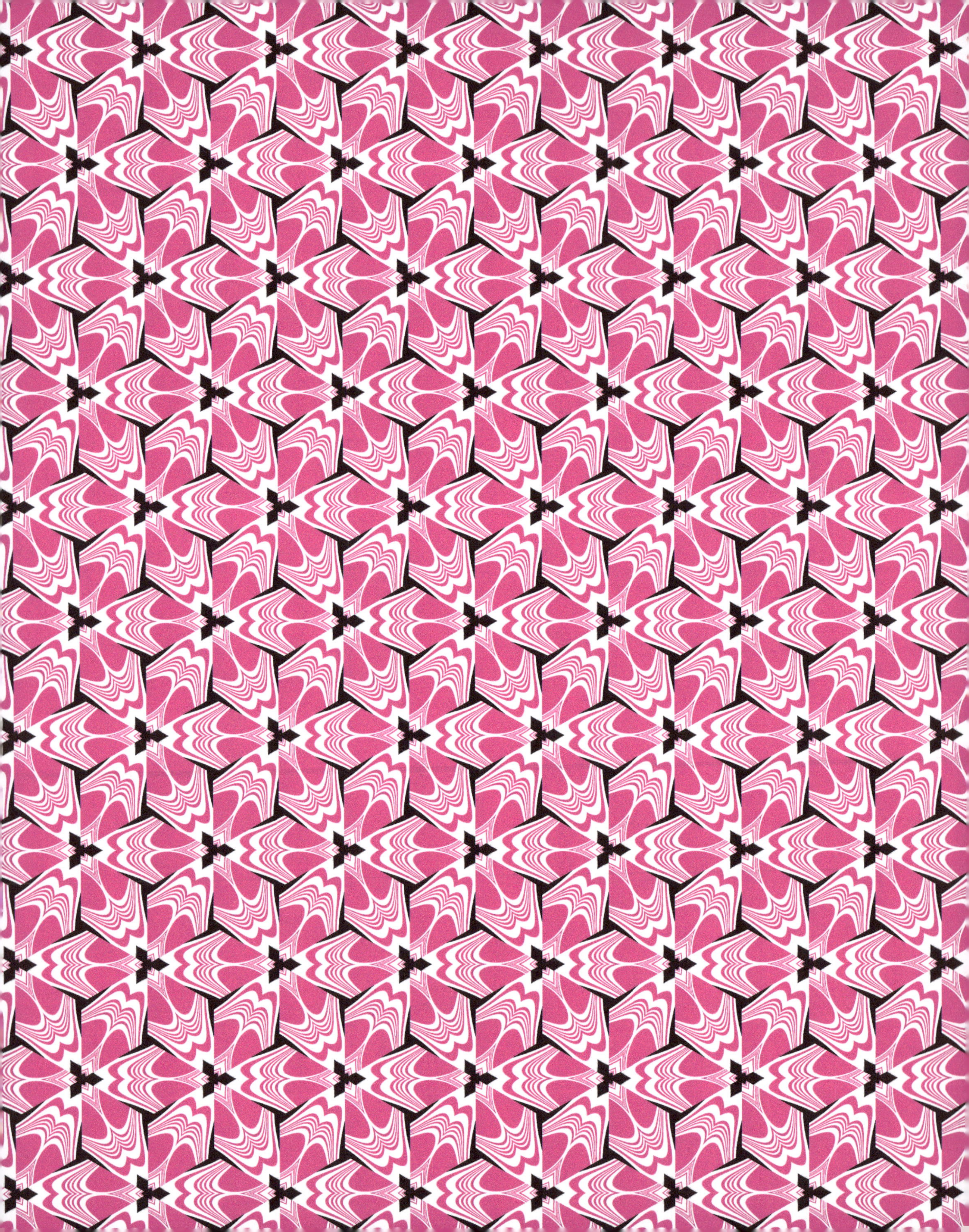

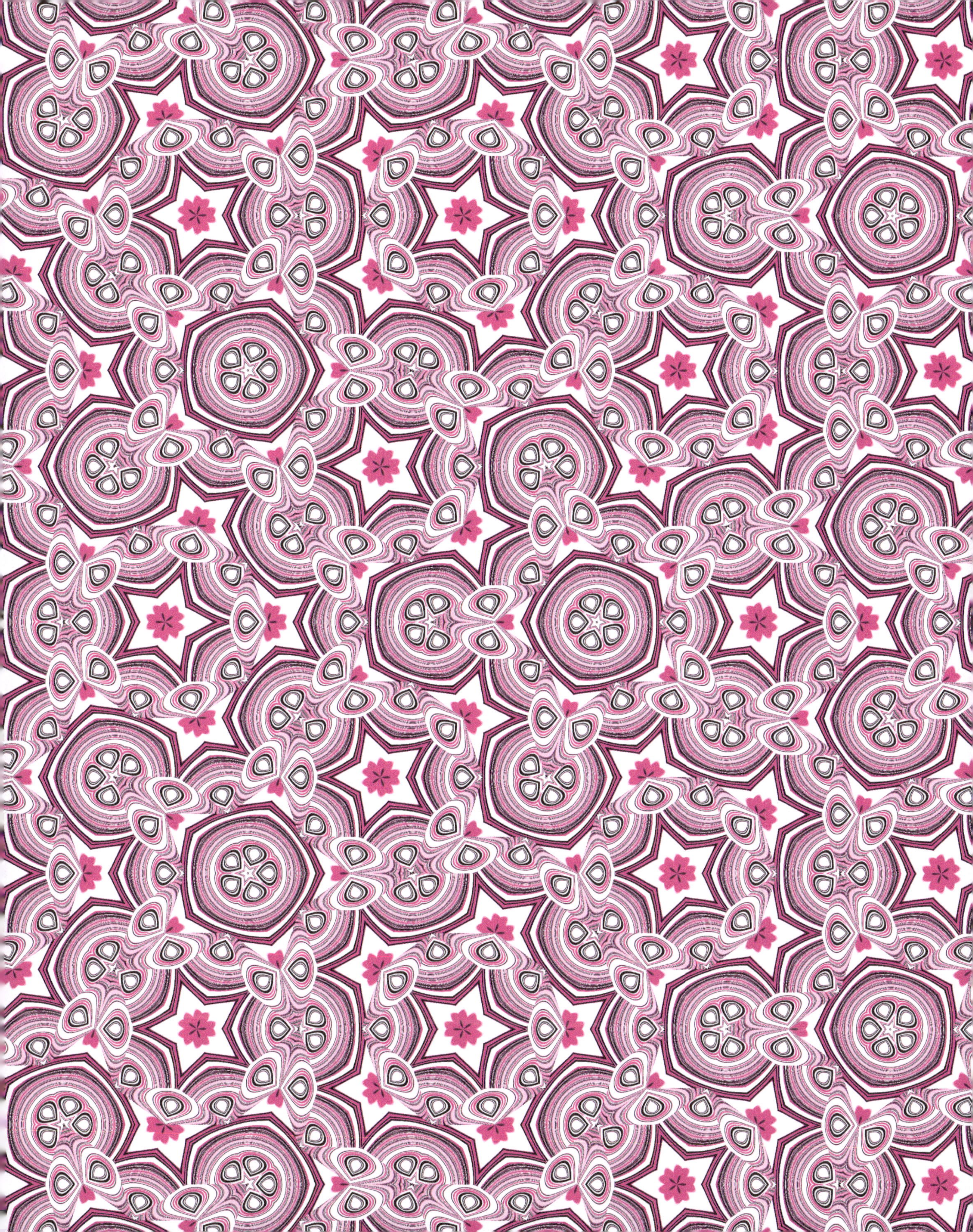

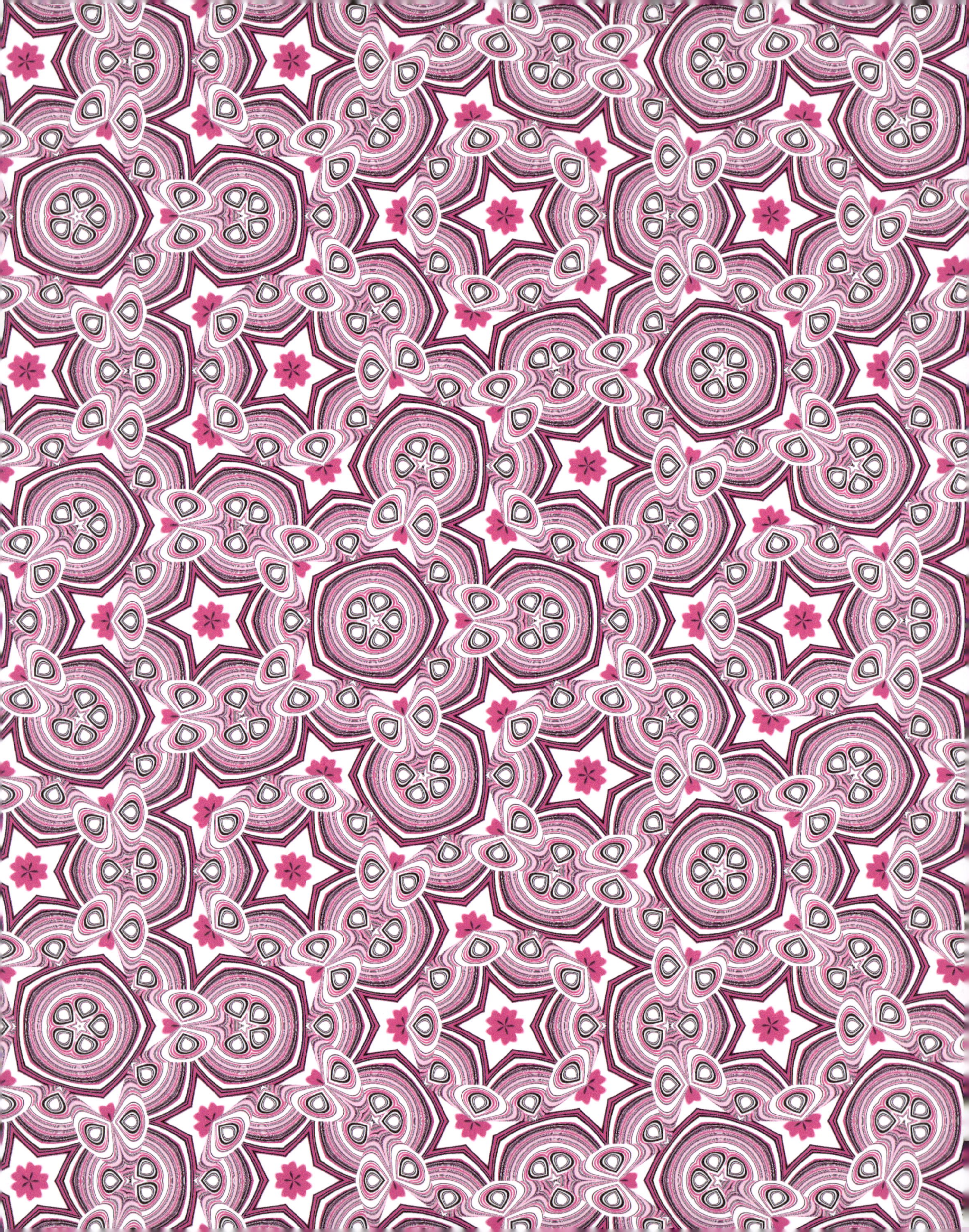

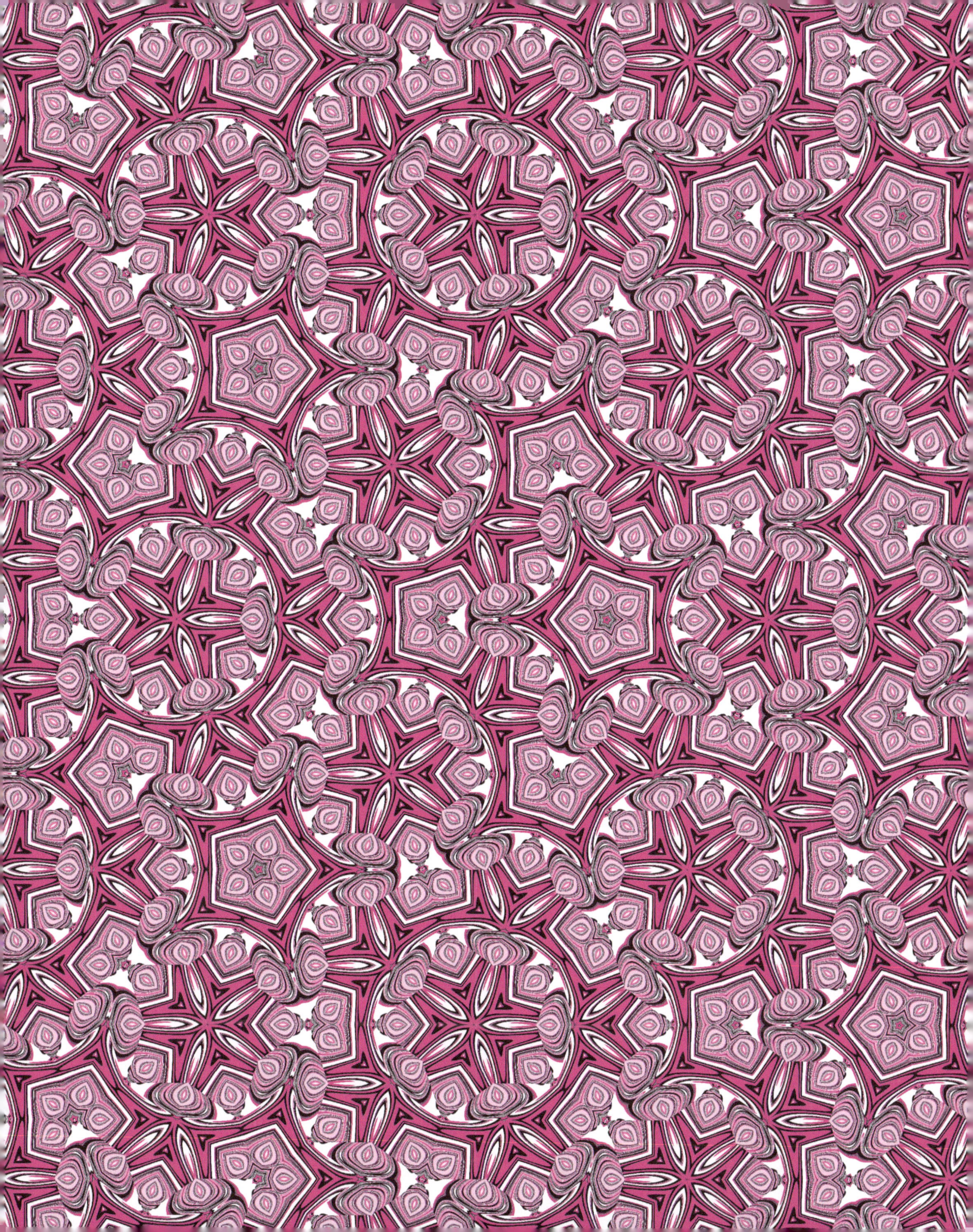

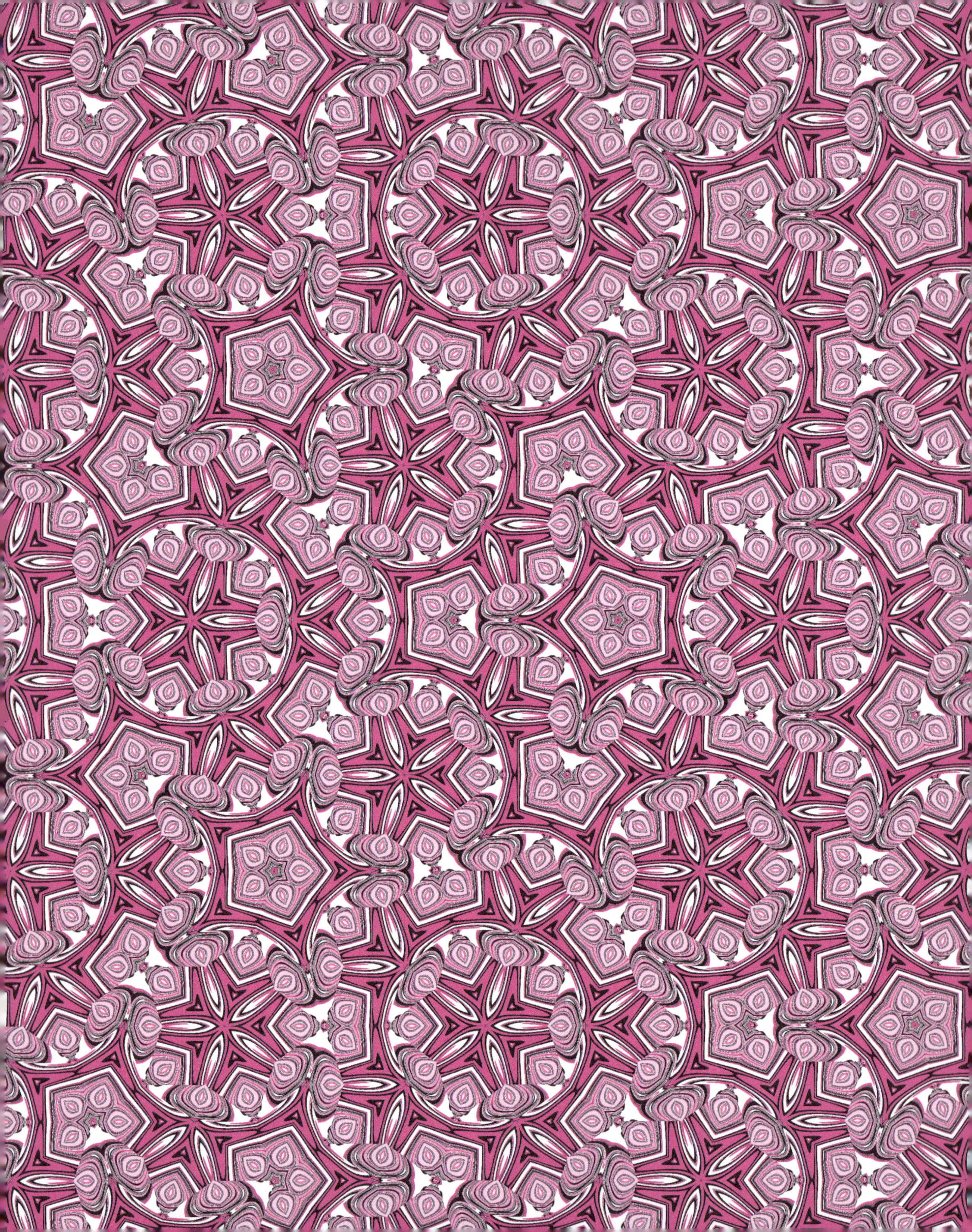

www.ingramcontent.com/pod-product-compliance
Lightning Source LLC
LaVergne TN
LVHW070156110826
845147LV00002B/417

* 9 7 8 1 9 4 7 1 5 8 2 0 7 *